Small Town VBS

...ebrations!

3 Vacation Bible School Programs with Small Town Heart and Big Time Ideas!

Short Stories

by
Gennifer Anderson
&
Sonja Toews

God's Most Wanted

TEACH Services, Inc.
PUBLISHING
www.TEACHServices.com

Copyright © 2013 TEACH Services, Inc.
ISBN-13: 978-1-57258-778-6 (Paperback)
ISBN-13: 978-1-57258-779-3 (Loose Leaf)
ISBN-13: 978-1-57258-789-0 (ePub)
ISBN-13: 978-1-57258-781-6 (Kindle / Mobi)

Library of Congress Control Number: 2012947532

Published by

TEACH Services, Inc.
P U B L I S H I N G
www.TEACHServices.com

Acknowledgements

Gennifer—Where to begin? I would like to thank: Jesus the Author of all; my family—Jeremy, Jadon, Seth, Toby, and two little Anderson babies waiting for Jesus—who has lived with my computer more than they wish for the sake of this project; my dad who lived and died loving Jesus, and my mom who lives loving and sharing Jesus every way she can; my sister, Heidi, who has made the skits funny, and my brothers, Peter and Elijah, who have offered advice (long before I asked); the family I married into; the wonderful VBS staff I have had the privilege to serve with; and my faithful friends and family who have cheered me on along God's path and prayed for me, especially Heidi Estrem Jorgenson and Rachel Anderson Drake for their ideas and prayers.

Sonja—Thanks to our gracious God for His wondrous presence in every aspect of our lives, including this project! To my husband, Bobby, and our two beautiful daughters, Lauren and Isabel. To my parents, who gave me my first foundation in the Lord and made God a priority in our home. To all of my family, including my husband's family, for their love and support. To Pastor Marty and the people of the Fargo SDA church who gave me my first loving introduction to the Adventist Church. To all of the friends God has blessed me with on my journey! He has placed so many wonderful people in my life at just the right time. I am thankful for each one!

Table of Contents

Introduction

The Story of How Two Crazy Girls Started Writing VBS Programs

So how do two local church girls (we use the term "girls" loosely since we are closer to thirty-something) end up writing VBS programs? Better yet, how do two full-time moms with part-time jobs find the time and energy to write one VBS program, let alone three? The short answer is God's motivation, inspiration, and guiding, along with the support of two wonderful husbands and an amazing church family.

We cannot possibly name all of the people that helped us with the VBS programs, but there are a few specific people that were instrumental in getting to the final stages of this project. Heidi Jorgenson, a school teacher and administrator, gave us the idea of presenting the story in three different formats to help ensure story retention. Gennifer's sister, Heidi Hanson, suggested using skits as the third story format. Kyle Anderson gave us all of our ideas and enthusiasm for decorating and setup.

For those of you who are interested, here is the long story of how we got involved in VBS and this project.

Gennifer

I grew up a Seventh-day Adventist in a town of 300 people. Our Adventist congregation was thirty miles away, and my family was often the only ones there with children. Each summer I attended VBS programs with friends at the local Church of the Nazarene in our small town. As an adult I still use some of the crafts I made as a child during VBS in our small town. My brother and I have talked on several occasions about how impressed we were with the crafts at the host church. I often think of the Church of the Nazarene with fondness.

This brings me to the major point of our programs—you never know the impact you are making on small children, so strive for long-term results, even in your crafts. If you can make bread or a birdhouse inexpensively, the memorable result is greater in many ways than a cheap craft made out of foam or paper.

In 2002 a friend asked me to help with our congregation's first VBS program using Group's Bug Safari. Working as the drama director was fun. Our entire VBS staff was made up of teens and young adults with the exception of two "older" adults. The program was high energy and fast-paced, which was a little shocking for our small Midwest church! Attendance topped out at forty-five children, which exceeded our expectations. That year we followed the program verbatim.

The next year our church hosted another Group VBS program, but we "tweaked" the snacks to less sugary foods. VBS had a huge staff change from the year before, and attendance was much smaller. I was a driving force behind planning VBS, and I served as drama director once again. I watched as the direction of our VBS program swept the shockwaves from the previous year into a strong dissatisfaction in our conservative congregation.

In 2004 we used yet another Group program but with disastrous results. Some staff outright quit, and attendance dropped to seventeen kids. One reason was that all the other churches around were doing the same program. Kids were going to churches closer to their home because most of the churches had the same program. I went home and looked online for the Bible village program I had remembered as a child. I found a site, but it was "locked" and under construction. I looked later and was routed to Group. Group had bought, revised, and marketed the Bible program for 2005. My interest was piqued, so I went to a VBS training program. Because of my new training (ha, ha), I was nominated the new VBS director for our church.

In 2005, 2006, and 2007 I helped implement Group's Bible village programs (Jerusalem, Galilee, and Bethlehem) in Minnesota and in California. (What? For real? Yes!) My dear friend Heidi from Minnesota was working at our little church school in California. When Heidi discovered that Week of Prayer at the church school coincided with spring break for the public school, we decided to host a VBS program at the church. So we brought the church school kids over and invited the community to learn more about Jesus, our church, and our school each morning. I liked those programs and the kids did, too. Our church family was supportive and had no worries about the programs. Attendance slowly grew.

In 2008 the Castles and Crowns VBS program from Review and Herald Publishing was introduced, and we tried it with great success. Our favorite part was the skits. Months later we were still hearing quotes and antidotes from those skits. We gratefully give credit to the creators of Castles and Crowns for giving us the skit ideas presented in these programs. Without the royal court, our VBS program would be missing something. (Note: Castles and Crowns program binder is full of information on staffing, child management, and many other organizational suggestions beyond the scope in this book. It is a wonderful resource, and the program is great, too.)

In 2009 I looked for another option but finally decided to try creating my own. I have a great interest in the biblical holy days and how they relate to our Adventist faith in particular. I thought VBS would be a fun way to introduce the biblical holy days, so I made a basic outline of my idea and asked a friend from church, Sonja Toews, to look it over. Sonja really helped make my ideas child friendly, and in the process she became highly involved with the planning. We were sure we had planned things down to the last inch. Then the night before VBS started I came down with a horrible latent flu bug! I was five months pregnant and had every symptom of misery available. I recovered enough to watch the last night. Sonja was quickly promoted to interim director, and since then she has never been able to move far from that position.

Sonja

I grew up in the Catholic Church where my parents laid the foundation of a firm Christian faith. I had never even heard of the Seventh-day Adventist Church until I met my high school sweetheart, who is now my husband, Bobby. He and his family were faithful church members, and they gave me a crash course in all things Adventist, including some new and interesting foods at potlucks! Bobby and I dated for four and a half years and then married while in college.

Our differing religious backgrounds convicted us that we needed to study and find God's truth for us and our future family. And study we did! We studied with folks from the Catholic Church and the Adventist Church. We attended both churches, and many others, in our quest for truth and family unity. God, of course, in His divine wisdom, had a plan in all of this, and at just the right time He brought a wonderful new pastor to the Fargo SDA Church.

Pastor Marty and his wife, Debbie, spoke to our hearts about the love of Jesus. God used them to draw us closer to Him and convict us of the truths of the Seventh-day Adventist Church. I was baptized into the church in 1999. Shortly after that time, I graduated from graduate school. Bobby had finished his schooling the year before. We moved to a small town of 700 people that was close to our families. I accepted my first job as a speech pathologist at a local school, and Bobby accepted a job at a large print company in a nearby town. I worked in the public school system for eleven years before deciding to work part time and start home schooling our daughters.

My husband and I, along with our two daughters, now attend the same local church that my husband grew up in. It is in this church that I met Gennifer, as well as other dear friends, who have continued to strengthen me in my walk with the Lord. This walk has taken me down paths I would have never expected, including my roles as a home school mom, Sabbath School teacher, and VBS leader. Although I certainly did not anticipate becoming so involved in those first original VBS programs, I will be forever grateful for this turn in my life. Working on VBS programs with Gennifer has never been "work" in the traditional sense. Gennifer has always had a contagious excitement for sharing God's love that is hard to resist! God has always been with us in our VBS planning times, continuously surprising us with new ideas and projects. Somehow, though, I am not totally surprised, for God has brought me many wonderful and unexpected gifts in my life. He truly has a plan for each of us!

As two crazy girls, we have become close friends, learning and growing together. It seems that God has brought us together for His glory, because what neither one of us could do alone, we do together, reaching beyond our wildest expectations to things God puts before us. God has also put a boundless desire in our hearts for sharing His love with the children in our church and in our community.

Our husbands, Jeremy and Bobby, have had to learn when to hide and when to stand firm before it involves them any further than they desire. Our husbands also know that we have a tendency to delve into various pursuits full-speed ahead when given the opportunity. We once picked 300 pounds of grapes in order to can jars upon jars of our special Sabbath grape juice, but that is another crazy story!

Our desire to share God's love with others gave us a desire to share the VBS ideas we had found worked for us with others. Our husbands thought this was crazy to say the least, but God loves working with crazy! A providential camp meeting encounter with a kind man in the publishing business eventually led to other doors opening in amazing ways until the completion of the publication you are reading now. So there you have it. That is the story of how two crazy girls started writing VBS programs!

We are hopeful that this is only the beginning of our story. God has watched over this effort and worked miracles in many ways while we have also seen Satan, God's archenemy, try to stall us. Prayers have overcome Satan's attempts, and we are pleased to offer this program to you for the glory of God.

We know God has a good and exciting plan for our lives, and we look forward to letting Him lead us on this adventure.

We want to wish you success and joy as you begin your own VBS journey! Perhaps you have been down the VBS road a time or two, or maybe this is your first experience leading a VBS program. Either way, our prayer is that these programs will bless each child and adult who takes part for many years to come!

Blessings,

Gennifer and Sonja

Notes:

Getting Started

This program is geared toward children ages five to twelve. However, with that said, we welcome anyone who comes. We don't think children are ever too small to be at VBS and doing some of the activities.

Some churches choose to have a baby class for those too small to interact on their own with the big group of older children. We didn't want to come up with a separate program nor did we have teachers for the smaller children—a wonderful alternative for our church was our teenage volunteers. Each teen was in charge of one or two children who were under age five. They helped "their" child do the actions to the songs, play the games, make the crafts, and eat their food, and, if need be, they let them just run around in a separate space set up for active little legs with the wiggles! It was a winning combination. The teens filled a very needed position and were so appreciated. And our small children learned to love Jesus, our church family, and VBS!

A note from Gennifer: I did not realize how much VBS mattered to very small ones until 2009 when I had an eight-month-old baby and was the director. Two of the teen girls at our church took turns watching Toby. They helped Toby do actions for the songs; they ran with Toby during games; and they kept Toby involved in every aspect that they could. Every day when I said it was time to go to VBS, Toby would grow very excited! Then VBS ended and life moved on.

Four months later Toby was learning to talk, and I could understand the sounds for Mama and Dada and his brothers, but there was one sound I just didn't know. It was one of the first sounds he had tried, and he kept trying. Finally, about a month after Toby's first try, I put the CD on from the summer's VBS program. Toby grew excited! And when the theme song came on—The B-I-B-L-E—Toby made the unidentified sound again. It was then that I realized what Toby had been trying to say all along—The B-I-B-L-E! It is still one of Toby's favorite words!

In regards to volunteers, for each section we tried to have a team consisting of at least a leader and a helper. Following is a suggested list of volunteers:

- Director and co-director

- Registration helpers (two people for the first night, one person to greet for the rest of the week)

- Song leader (one or two people; it helps to have one person focused on actions and one person primarily focused on lyrics)

- Craft leader and helper

- Game leader and helper

- Helpers for younger children (teens and grandparents make excellent candidates; you need one helper for every one to two children depending on the ages and needs of the children)

- Kitchen director and one to two helpers

- Drama (three key players with two or three extras)

It is also nice to have an "extra" person available to run errands and fill in where needed. This was the person who, for example, ran to the store for extra food.

Another important aspect of your program is the nightly schedule. The program is scheduled to last approximately 1 hour and 30 minutes. Following is a schedule with the recommended allotted times per activity. A five-minute transition time is accounted for within the times given. Your actual transition time may be more or less, depending on your group. Each activity will be explained as you read through the book.

Start Time	Activity	Total Minutes
6:00	Opening prayer Singing Bible story Prayer	10 minutes
6:10	Crafts	25 minutes
6:35	Suppertime Storytime	30 minutes
7:05	Games	15 minutes
7:20	Singing Skit Gum and Balloons Closing Prayer	15 minutes

Registration

Even if you know all the kids and adults, registration is still an important step that you don't want to ignore. The three reasons to collect information are:

1. **Emergency and allergy information** – Maybe you know Sally's mom's phone number, but does everybody on your VBS staff have her number in case of an emergency? What about Gary or Samantha or Sara or Tyler's parents? Having emergency contact information for each of the children attending your VBS program is crucial in today's society. Also, you will want to learn if any of the children have allergies, especially food allergies. By having this information, you will make the parents and staff members feel at ease, knowing that there is a plan in place in case of an emergency.

2. **Contact for other events** – We don't use this as much as it could be used, but here are some ideas we have implemented:

   a. VBS follow-up communication: Print a group picture or favorite shot from the week, maybe of the Royal Court for instance, to give to each child. Include a handwritten note on the back, such as "Had a great time with you at VBS! See you next year!"

   b. Invitation to other church events: If you are doing another children's event at your church, use the VBS contact information you have to invite the children from the community. This is a great way to have them interact with your church throughout the year.

   c. Birthday cards: We have sent birthday cards to the children. This makes them feel special and valued, which endears them to your church even more.

   d. VBS invitation: Of course, make sure you personally invite them to next year's VBS program when the summer rolls around again.

3. **VBS planning for the next year** – You think you will remember how many children attended. You think you will remember if you had about the same number of boys as girls. You might, but you might not. If you collect the registration information, you will have all the information you need when you begin planning the next year's program. And even if you don't serve as director, you will be helping the new person get a jump start on planning. This information especially comes in handy when ordering supplies. We review last year's attendance and factor in the changes we know of to make planning easier.

We found parents who we were familiar with tended to skip writing down some of the information. Stress to parents that it's worth writing it down for VBS because the staff may need it in the case of an emergency. See Emergency Contact Form

If you choose, you can add the registration information into your computer. That way you can keep the records and review them for returning children the next year. This can speed up the registration process in subsequent years if you just have parents verify that all of their information is still correct. You can then add new children and/or update information that has changed for those who previously attended.

Emergency Contact Form

Child's Name: _____

Child's Birthday (example 9/21/81): _____

Child's Address: _____

Child's Parents/Guardians: _____

Parent's Emergency Phone Number: _____

Allergies (food or medication) or other medical information needed: _____

_____

_____

Decorations

You can get very elaborate with your decorations, or you can choose a simple design. The most important thing is to pull together kid-friendly decorations that will brighten your church and create a festive atmosphere during VBS.

For simplicity and unity, we chose to go with a theme of colors for each of the three programs. We used the colors red and orange for Celebrations, red and green for Short Stories, and red and black for God's Most Wanted. We hung up balloons and party streamers in the main room and draped bright solid colored flags around the room to add a splash of color. For the craft area, we covered the tables in inexpensive plastic tablecloths in our theme colors.

Designate an area for the opening and closing program and the skits. In each program's section, you will find more theme-specific ideas, but the skit normally takes center stage, and so do its decorations. For the throne room, we used a big oversized chair from the parent's room and draped it with nice fabric for the queen. For the king, we found an old wooden chair with a high back and spray painted it gold. In the skit area we also had a big jar, wooden barrel, or another large container of interest to put about a gallon of bubble gum in, which we refilled as needed every night.

Not only did we use the balloons as decorations, but we used them as a learning tool. We hung a string of balloons, each one with a small question inside on a paper slip, such as "What was the story about tonight?", "What did you learn tonight?", etc. The queen had a thumbtack taped on the end of her scepter, and each evening she allowed five children to pop a different balloon. Then each child had to answer the question in the balloon they popped. If the child was younger, a general answer was accepted. For example, if the question was "Where was our story found?", we would accept the answer "the Bible." If the child was older, the expectation was a more specific answer. Because the goal of the exercise is to encourage learning and the correct answer, we allowed children to ask for help from friends in their group. If they answered the question correctly, they got to take a handful out of the bubble gum jar.

We worried about this idea for many reasons, but we decided that we could always quit if it started to become a problem. It was wonderful! The joy in popping a balloon with everybody watching was enough incentive for the kids to pay careful attention to the details of the Bible story throughout the evening. The kids shared easily, and with the promise of a turn for everybody before the week was out and a chance to help with the questions, there was a joyful exuberance in the room when we popped the balloons each evening. Overall, this was a greatly enjoyed part of the program, and the kids loved the reward. This total strategy achieved our goal in a visible way, and we highly recommend it! Try it once, if it doesn't work, you can always stop! But we think you will enjoy it as much as we did.

> *A note from Sonja*: Decorations are a wonderful way to create excitement in children. We were blessed with several volunteers who worked hard to create a perfect environment for VBS. Our space was limited, and we had to be creative with our resources, but the end result was amazing each year! Gennifer's brother-in-law, Kyle, was indispensible when it came to decorating. He could take an old sheet, a misplaced chair, and a few streamers, and turn them into a royal courtyard with the blink of an eye! Look for people in your church family who enjoy decorating, and ask if they would be willing to help set the scene for your week.

Story Presentation

We found our children didn't care to do worksheets or watch TV to "learn" the stories at VBS. We wanted stories for the kids to enjoy and learn from, so we looked for better options. Following is what worked for us:

- **Story Presentation One** – This is the children's first introduction to the story at the beginning of the program. I brought in a vintage suitcase with clues packed in it and my dad's beautiful leather-bound Bible. The suitcase helped add suspense, since the children were curious about what was inside. After opening the suitcase and going through the clues, I read that night's story out of the Bible while producing clues or props from the suitcase, stopping to explain anything difficult to the children.

- **Story Presentation Two** – During the mealtime between the main course and dessert, while it was a little calmer, we read that night's Bible story out of a book, showing the children the pictures. Even the older children found it interesting, and the smaller children loved it!

- **Story Presentation Three** – During the closing program, the Bible story is brought up again in the skit in a different context. Then at the end we tested the kids' knowledge with the balloon game. The audience and drama team loved the skits. I have no idea who ended up having the most fun!

A note from Gennifer: For three years we had a young girl who volunteered to play the part of the queen's assistant. The year of God's Most Wanted, I finally wrote her into the script. It is a perfect place to use young preteens or others who want to participate but don't want a starring role. Look for this type of opportunity to maximize participation in VBS.

We did not introduce Bible verses for the children to memorize each day. One verse would easily be appropriate, but five verses, one for each evening, felt unreasonable for long-term results. We also never found a real smooth way of adding that part into our program, so we never incorporated it. If you find a way to do it, let us know!

Treasures and Surprises

Our 2009 VBS program incorporated a treasure keeper who dispersed special treasures each night at the end of VBS. This idea came about in an effort to make VBS exciting and memorable, and boy did it work! Gennifer's brother, Peter, served as our treasure keeper. He fit the bill perfectly with his tall stature and kind attitude. Each night the children looked forward to the treasure keeper opening his big chest of treasures and giving them each something special.

Because of the relatively small number of children in attendance, as well as donations from church members, we were able to give beautiful gifts to the children each night. The gifts included CDs with VBS music, special homemade blankets, hand-crafted wooden breadboards, and finally a Bible of their very own on the last night.

A note from Sonja: My children, as well as the neighbor children who came with us to VBS, still refer to Peter as the "treasure keeper" almost three years later! He certainly made an impression on them!

We continue to see the special treasures, including the Bibles, arrive with children for Sabbath School and church services.

We have worked some aspect of the special treasures into each VBS program. Look for ideas in each program's setup information, and then add your own gift ideas to the program as suits your children and congregation. You may find that you have members who are more than willing to make a donation of their time, money, or talents for this cause. Perhaps a lady from your church would love to make each child a special pillow, blanket, or decoration. Maybe there is a gentleman who could use his carpentry skills to carve out treasure boxes or breadboards. Consider the long-term impact these gifts will make and decide what is right for your church.

A single gift at the close of VBS is certainly another option. Even if you opt not to give gifts, you can still make VBS special and memorable through your crafts, songs, food, and the caring attitude of your staff members.

Music

We have tried doing music a variety of ways, but we have decided that the most important part is the song leader's willingness to involve the children. You can use a piano or guitar, old hymns or new praise songs. Action songs *are* better than stoical sitting, even if you need to create your own actions. On key or tone deaf voices will not matter much to small children when compared to the ability to connect and hold their interest. Of course, if you can find a person who sings nicely, the rest of the VBS staff will be grateful!

Canned music was helpful for us, especially when learning new songs. Shopping online was a good option for us because we could hear samples of the music and take our time shopping while our small children played around our feet. If you have a song in mind and just need a sound track, Amazon.com, MP3 format section, is pretty good. Just type in the name of the song and listen to the samples provided to find the song and sound you are looking for. You can then buy with a debit or credit card and it uploads to your computer. (Amazon is a secular web site, and we are not recommending the contents of the whole site in anyway).

In addition, Creative Ministry Solutions (http://www.creativemin.com) has a lot of Christian music and puppetry resources for sale. They offer a nice selection of fun songs and albums, some with themed CD's. You may be able to receive a bulk discount, too, when buying large quantities. It never hurts to ask. We received a bulk discount from One Way Street, Inc., which was bought out by Creative Ministry Solutions.

Another great option is Miss Brenda and the Kids' Time Singers CDs available from Chapel Music and the Adventist Book Center. There is a huge variety of songs available, and the words and tunes are very easy to sing with! You can listen to sound clips or download songs at Chapel Music's Web site (http://www.chapelmusic.com).

For each program, you will find suggested songs that we used for the opening and closing program each evening. For the Celebrations and God's Most Wanted programs, the songs came from a CD titled *Celebrate Jesus!* by Concordia Publishing House. For the Short Stories program, we found "The B-I-B-L-E" and "The Shrink Song" on a CD titled *Little Praise Party: My Best Friend* by Yancy Ministries, Inc. The songs are also available individually on Amazon. *Little Praise Party* did draw some deserved criticism over the cover art and harder rock sound contained in unused parts of the album.

"The Shrink Song" can also be sung to the tune of "Fishers of Men" on Miss Brenda and the Kids' Time Singers. The words for the song are as follows. Begin standing up and repeat given motions at appropriate times.

The Shrink Song

If you neglect your Bible *(have hands open and up but push away)*

Forget to pray *(hands together and drop down)*

Forget to pray

Forget to pray

If you neglect your Bible

Forget to pray

Then you'll shrink, shrink, shrink

(sink down lower and lower until you are laying flat on the floor)

Then you'll shrink, shrink, shrink

Then you'll shrink, shrink, shrink

If you neglect your Bible

Forget to pray

Then you'll shrink, shrink, shrink

But if you read your Bible *(hands together and open)*

Pray every day *(hands together)*

Pray every day

Pray every day

If you read your Bible

Pray every day

Then you'll grow, grow, grow

(start low and grow slow; you have to grow a long way)

Then you'll grow, grow, grow

Then you'll grow, grow, grow

If you read your Bible

Pray everyday

Then you'll grow, grow, grow

Crafts

For the craft area, we recommend setting up tables with no chairs. This provides plenty of space to work and extra space to move about. Cover the tables with inexpensive tablecloths. Just remember, each child needs enough room for their elbows to move! In general, begin with the children standing around the craft table.

It is nice to have a sample of each completed craft, which can be made earlier by the instructor. This is helpful for the children and the volunteers who are helping the kids.

You can explain the main point of the craft at the beginning of the craft time or while the children work quietly, giving them the needed details each step of the way. Do what works well for your group.

Always start with the children putting their name on their project! Put common supplies, such as markers, crayons, scissors, glue, paint, etc., for the day in the center of each table for easy access.

We tried really hard to maximize our efforts and create an impression with the children and the adults. Quality and variety played a big part in our craft selections.

Food Preparation

To us, food and meals are important enough to plan around, and VBS is no exception. We hold our VBS program in the evening, so we felt it was invaluable to include supper in our plans so that families don't have to rush and parents can bring their children to VBS without worrying about supper. We hope this removes a barrier for busy parents who may not enroll their children because of their schedules.

The first year we did VBS our staff was made up of mostly young adults, so we planned a potluck supper each evening before VBS. Something like spaghetti—someone bring red sauce, someone bring noodles, someone else bring garlic bread. It gave us a time to connect, review the plans for the evening, and evaluate the VBS program thus far, and it was fun! We served the suggested snack to the kids in the middle of the program and that worked well.

The next year our staff changed to mostly parents with small children and adults with full-time jobs. Making supper before VBS was really hard, and the VBS "snack time" became supper for quite a few children and staff.

The next year we decided to try a complete, yet simple, meal in place of the snack and serve it earlier in the program. That was a huge success! Our staff was more on time, and they were not starving during VBS! Strangely, my VBS food team said the cost was about the same as the "snack" before, and they felt that the food preparation didn't take any longer.

Each day we selected a variety of food options that were both healthy and fun. In addition to the main dish, add veggies or fruit as a side for each evening. Carrot or celery sticks with ranch dressing or apples, grapes, strawberries, bananas, or melons will round out the meal. You can tailor these options to meet the needs of your group. Most of the children were very happy with the food offered, even without previous introductions to different food.

Having one or two people willing to take charge of food preparation and serving is very helpful. We had one wonderful woman who *asked* if she could coordinate people to bring desserts for each night. Desserts can be homemade or store bought. Simple is easy. Cookies, rice crispy bars, or fruit crisps all work great! There are a few specific suggestions for some of the nights, but otherwise, pick your favorite dessert and go with it!

We served water with our meals. It was easy, inexpensive, and not hard to clean up after. And after all the movement, the children needed to be rehydrated!

If a snack is preferred to a whole meal, we recommend choosing healthy food combinations such as carrot sticks, apple slices, grapes, bananas with wheat crackers, pretzels, fresh bread, etc. If you want to go the dairy route, try adding in cheese slices, string cheese, or go-gurt packs , too.

A note from Gennifer and Sonja: We know all about food allergies! Well, not really, but a lot more than we had ever thought we would after multiple life-altering diagnoses in our families. You can easily alter the suggested foods and make substitutions as needed to work with those children and adults with food allergies.

Special Sabbath Program

We plan Sabbath as a day to show off what we have done all week. We like to leave our decorations up for Sabbath and take them down on Sunday so our church family can experience a piece of the fun and excitement of the week. We work with those in charge of the church service and arrange to tell the children's story, sing for special music, and talk about what we've done during a special time in the service.

We actually let the kids vote for their favorite skit on Friday, and then we present it again on Sabbath for children's story. We perform our theme song for special music. During another allotted portion of the service, we present a slide show of pictures from the week while VBS music plays in the background.

Because the classrooms are full of VBS stuff and the children have been used to such a different schedule, we have found that it works well to have breakfast on Sabbath morning with the kids, parents, and staff. This way everyone gets to hang out and visit together.

A note from Gennifer: Prepare a yummy Sabbath pancake breakfast! Top with syrup, peanut butter, and/or applesauce. You can buy a pancake mix or make them from scratch.

Pancakes

2 cups flour	2 tablespoons sugar
½ teaspoon salt	1 egg
1 teaspoon baking soda	¼ cup oil
2 teaspoons baking powder	2 cups water

Mix dry ingredients together, then add wet ingredients and mix well. Pour a ¼ cup of batter onto a hot skillet and flip when bubbles appear. Serve warm!

We have even added a game to play after the morning brunch, although this is optional. The reason for the game is to present the idea that Sabbath is a little part of heaven with treasures waiting to be discovered!

Purchase or make a piñata. A piñata can also be purchased from Oriental Trading or a local party store. Or make your own. To construct a smaller piñata, simply use an old cereal box and follow these directions:

1. Fill empty cereal box with treats.
2. Seal shut with heavy-duty tape.
3. Punch two holes on top and run a long string through to hang the piñata.
4. Cut apart tissue paper of various colors and glue to the outside of the box to make the desired pattern.
5. Add streamers or other embellishments.

Fill the piñata with Bible verse pencils, rubber bouncy balls, bookmarks, candy, and whatever else you can find as a last treat for the children.

Hang the piñata in an appropriate spot. Allow younger kids to go first and swing a plastic or soft bat. Have the children take turns until the piñata breaks. (A parent may need to hit the piñata with a regular bat to make the first break or get the last of the candy to fall.)

Supply paper lunch bags for the kids to put their treasures in. After the game, encourage the children to make sure other children have a fair share and to keep their bag in their vehicle during church time.

Notes:

Program 1

Celebrations!

Looking Forward by Looking Back

Daily Schedule

	Day One	Day Two	Day Three	Day Four	Day Five
Theme	Passover	Unleavened Bread/First Fruits	Feast of Weeks/ Pentecost	Trumpets/Day of Atonement	Tabernacles
Main Point	Saved for life!	The stuff of life!	Proof of life!	Sharing life!	The good life!
Bible Story*	Exodus and Christ's death	Christ's resurrection and return to heaven	Ten Commandments and work of the Holy Spirit	Our witness and Christ's return	Heaven
Crafts	Remembrance plate	Personalized aprons	Sweet bread	Memory book and candles	Beaded key ring
Food	Lentils and flat bread	Burritos	Potatoes and cornbread	Hot dogs, baked beans, s'mores	Pizza and cupcakes or angel food cake
Storytime	*Celebrations!* (Passover section)	*Celebrations!* (traveling, first fruits section)	*Celebrations!* (later fruits section)	*Celebrations!* (trumpets/Day of Atonement section)	*Celebrations!* (tabernacles section)
Games	Barefoot Tag	Hide and Seek	Relay Race	Red Rover	"Moving Camp"
Skit	Saved for life!	The stuff of life!	Proof of life!	Sharing life!	The good life!

A note from Gennifer and Sonja: In the other two programs, we give you specific Bible texts as your sole reference for the first presentation of the stories. However, in Celebrations! we suggest that you use the storybook by Gennifer titled *Celebrations!* for this section in addition to or in place of direct Bible readings. *Celebrations!* provides a simplified version of more complicated stories. We feel that with this more detailed topic, using the storybook helps bring the main points to a child's level. For the second story reading, we liked using *The Young Readers Bible* by Bonnie Bruno and Carol Reinsma..

Opening Program

Day One — Passover

Bible Story and Main Point:

- Exodus—Saved for life
- Christ's death—Saved for life

Story Props:

- Bible
- Sheep
- Cross

Songs:

- "Hope's Celebration"
- "Crayon Box Song" (Miss Brenda Kids' Time Singers)

Day Two — Unleavened Bread/First Fruits

Bible Story and Main Point:

- Christ's resurrection—Stuff of life
- Christ's ascension—Stuff of life

Story Props:

- Picture of Christ's empty tomb
- Cracker to represent flat bread

Songs:

- "Hope's Celebration"
- "This is the Day" (Miss Brenda and Kids' Time Singers)
- "When I Remember" (Miss Brenda and Kids' Time Singers)

Day Three — Feast of Weeks/Pentecost

Bible Story and Main Point:

- Ten Commandments—Proof of life
- Work of the Holy Spirit—Proof of life

Story Props:

- Ten Commandment emblem
- Holy Spirit emblem, such as a ceramic dove

Songs:

- "These Things Are Written"
- "Pass It On" (Miss Brenda and Kids' Time Singers)
- "Give Me Oil" (Miss Brenda and Kids' Time Singers)

Day Four — Trumpets/Day of Atonement

Bible Story and Main Point:

- Our witness—Sharing life
- Christ's return—Sharing life

Story Props:

- Trumpet, real or a toy
- Picture of Christ's return

Songs:

- "Now That You Know"
- "Soon and Very Soon" (Miss Brenda and Kids' Time Singers)

Day Five — Tabernacles

Bible Story and Main Point:

- Heaven—The good life

Story Props:

- Something to represent camping, such as tent stakes or a small toy tent
- Something to represent heaven, such as a picture

Songs:

- "I Shall Dwell in the House of the Lord Forever"
- "I'm Gonna Sing" (Miss Brenda and Kids' Time Singers)

Crafts

Day One — Remembrance Plate

Materials:

- Solid colored clear plastic or glass plates (one for each child; available at large retail or dollar-type stores)
- Permanent paint pens in multiple colors

Instructions:

Give each child a plate and instruct them to write their name on the plate. Then let the children decorate the plate however they wish until the end of the craft time. This project will need at least a day to dry before going home with the children. Make sure you have a place where the plates can dry without little fingers touching them.

Explanation:

This week is about celebrations! Tonight is a time to remember that with Jesus we are saved for life, and because of Him, tonight is a celebration of freedom from our sins. We are going to make a special plate for you to use for celebrations. When you use this plate, you will remember lots of celebrations, especially tonight when we talked about being saved for life!

Day Two — Personalized Aprons

Materials:

- Canvas aprons (one for each child; available from Oriental Trading, craft stores, and some large retail stores)
- Fabric paints

Instructions:

Give each child an apron. Have them write their name somewhere on it (most children will use their name as part of the decoration). Let them decorate their apron until craft time is done. Leave aprons to dry in a secure location free of possible paint interference!

Explanation:

Food and water—those are the things we think about when we think about stuff we need for life! We need air, too, but we don't normally need to think about that. Above all, we need Jesus for life—eternal life! Jesus says He is the Living Bread and Water. Bread and water were the main meals during Bible times. They were the basis for survival. Jesus is the stuff of life for us. We need Him for eternal life. Today we are going to make an apron for when you make the stuff of life, and when you cook, we want to remember that Jesus is the stuff of life!

Day Three — Sweet Bread

Materials:

- Paper lunch bags (one for each child)

- Toothpick flags (one for each child; a strip of white masking tape three inches long folded in half over a toothpick makes a flag. Make these before VBS starts, if possible!)

- Cooking spray

- Bread dough (you can buy it in the freezer section and thaw it out earlier that day, or you can make it fresh; plan on about a lemon-sized ball of dough for each child).

- Cinnamon/sugar mixture in shakers

- Raisins and chocolate chips to decorate with

Instructions:

The children should wash their hands before coming in to do this craft. The children should first write their name on a tape flag and paper bag and place it in front of their workstation. Next they should hold their hands out, palms up. Spray a light coating of cooking spray on each child's hands. Then give each child a ball of bread dough.

Let each child use the remainder of the class time crafting their very own loaf of bread. When the craft time is about over, have each child place their loaf on a baking sheet with their tape flag sticking out of it. Bake the bread in a preheated oven at 350 degrees for 15 minutes. Cool for five minutes and place in marked bags for the children to take home after the closing program.

Explanation:

Jesus gives us proof of life! We are saved for life, and Jesus is our stuff of life—we need Him for everything. We are learning today about the Ten Commandments. God gave us these so we would know what proof of life looks like. In bread, like we are going to make today, the yeast is the life of the bread, but it doesn't work or make the bread grow without sweetness. The Holy Spirit is the sweetness to our proof of life! We need all the ingredients in our life and our bread to make things just right!

Sonja's Amish White Bread

2 cups warm water (110° F)

⅔ cup granulated sugar

1 ½ tablespoons active dry yeast

1 ½ teaspoons salt

¼ cup vegetable oil

6 cups flour

Dissolve sugar into the water. Stir in the yeast, and proof until creamy foam appears. Add salt and oil, and mix. Add one cup of flour at a time while continuing to mix. Knead the dough once all the flour is added. Store covered in the refrigerator for up to 24 hours until desired use time.

Day Four — Memory Book and Candles

Memory Book

Materials:

- Small photo album book, approximately 24 pages (one for each child; often a dollar store will have nicely decorated photo books or many large retail stores with photo sections also carry a small inexpensive photo book).

- 4 x 6 index cards (at least five for each child)

- Colored pens/markers and stickers

Instructions:

Give each child a photo book and five cards. They should write their name on their book and make sure the cards stay with the book when finished. Each child should decorate and/ or write on the cards things Jesus has done for them. This is a good time for adult or teen leaders to help with spelling or brainstorming! If the cover of the photo book needs embellishments, the children can also decorate that.

Explanation:

We have a Rescuer who wants us to share life with others! Jesus is sharing life with us now and in heaven, and He wants us to follow His example. The best way to do that is to share with others how Jesus has worked in our lives; we need to share our story. Today we are going to make some special cards that will help us remember the things Jesus has done for us. We can use these cards to help tell about His work in our lives. What has Jesus done for you? Think of some special times Jesus has worked in your life.

Candles

Materials:

- Taper candles (two for each child)
- Glitter puff paint in bottles
- Buckets
- Sand

Instructions:

The photo books should be placed in a safe location before beginning this project. You will want to make sure the craft table is covered securely with something you don't mind getting paint on. Give each child a candle and place puff paint on the table, enough so that each child can have one bottle. The kids can decorate the candles with dots, swirls, stripes, etc. Stand candles in the sand-filled buckets to let the paint dry.

Explanation:

When sharing life sometimes we say we are letting our light shine. Today we are going to make some lights to share with our church family on Sabbath. The Sabbath is such a special day to celebrate Jesus' love for us. We have been learning all week about special ways to remember God. We've learned about the Bible's holy days as ways to remember God and all He's done and will do for us. We have made and received special gifts that will help us remember God. Today we are going to make special candles to help us remember God and celebrate Sabbath.

Day Five — Beaded Key Ring

Materials:

- Leather lacing, yarn, or thicker string

- Pony beads (can be purchased in the craft section of large retail stores or from Oriental Trading)

- Key rings (can be purchased in the craft section of large retail stores or from Oriental Trading)

Instructions:

Each child should select a handful of beads. Younger children can place beads in a single line on the string and have an adult/helper tie the last bead on each end to secure it. Older children can make their key ring into the shape of a cross. There are many variations of beaded cross crafts available online and in craft books. Below is a simple variation adapted from ehow.com. It is a good idea to make a sample of this craft ahead of time so that you know the steps.

1. Fold the lacing in half to find the exact middle. Slide one pony bead onto the cord and place it in the middle spot.
2. Pull the two sides of the laces together. Place four pony beads over both of the laces. This makes the base of the cross. Separate the two cords.
3. Slide two beads on each side of the cord. Run the cord through the middle of one bead while it is turned sideways. Repeat this on the other cord. Feed the cord back through the other two beads on both leather strips.
4. Pull both sides of the leather tight. Place three beads on the leather strips with both sides running through the beads. Tie a knot in the leather to hold the cross into place.
5. Tie the two leather laces to the key ring to complete the craft.

Explanation:

Jesus is making a good life for us in heaven. All of our celebrations are looking forward to one big celebration in heaven! We are going to make a beautiful key chain that will remind us of the home Jesus is preparing for us in heaven, where we will enjoy the good life!

Day One — Lentils, bread or crackers, veggies, and dessert

A note from Gennifer: For some reason I have always thought of lentil soup as a Bible food and especially connected to Passover, so I asked my mother-in-law to make her special soup for the Celebration program. You can buy flat bread, crackers, or corn chips to go with the soup, or you can make your own. This is a great time to introduce and use what we call communion bread, if desired.

Christine's Lentil Soup (serves 12-15)

1 package lentils	2 teaspoons salt
3 ribs celery	¼ teaspoon oregano
3 carrots	½ tablespoon powdered
1 onion	chicken seasoning
2 quarts water	Soymilk powder (not vanilla) or
¼ teaspoon thyme	1 pint half and half

Rinse the lentils, and put them in a pot. Blender the celery, carrots, and onion with some of the water. Pour the liquid mixture into the pot. Add the rest of the water and seasonings. Cook about 45 minutes or until tender. Turn heat off and add milk-type ingredient. The lentils are also good served with salsa.

Unleavened Bread

½ cup olive oil   Pinch of salt

½ cup water   2 cups whole wheat flour

Preheat the oven to 350 degrees. Combine the olive oil, water, and salt. Wisk it until it's near-frothy white. Alternatively, you can put it in a blender instead. Loosely mix in the flour until blended. You don't want to mix it too much. Make sure the dough is the same consistency of a drier batch of cookie dough.

Make dough balls the size of a golf ball, flatten them, score them with a knife, and pierce them with a dinner fork in the shape of a cross. Sprinkle the top with salt from a table shaker, if desired. Bake for about 10 minutes. Watch it constantly after 9 minutes to avoid burning. Browned (not just burnt) communion bread tastes bitter. Adjust the time for crispier or flimsier bread.

Whole Wheat Crackers

½ teaspoon salt   1 cup whole wheat flour

2 tablespoons Brewers yeast   1 cup quick oats

1 tablespoon brown sugar   ½ teaspoon vanilla

¼ cup sunflower seeds   ½ cup oil

¼ cup sesame seed   ½ cup water

⅔ cup chopped nuts

⅔ cup soy flour

Roll the dough between two sheets of wax paper. Put on pan, score, and bake at 300 degrees for 20-25 minutes.

Day Two — Burritos and dessert

A note from Gennifer: Bean burritos are an easy and filling meal, and kids love filling tortilla wraps with the fillings they choose! Just have everything in an assembly line, and you are good to go.

Flour tortillas (we had both large and small sizes available, which were warmed)

Refried beans (we bought the no-fat refried beans in the can and served them warm)

Cheese, shredded

Lettuce, shredded

Tomatoes, diced

Green onions, cut

Black olives, sliced

Sour cream

Salsa

Avocados or guacamole

Day Three — Potatoes, cornbread, and dessert

A note from Gennifer: You can bake or boil the potatoes. Our staff thought boiling them was easier. We used many of the leftovers from the previous meal idea to make a potato bar.

Cornbread is a great addition to this meal. Following is my all-time favorite cornbread recipe from my brother, Peter, who loves to make things special. Mini cornbread muffins are easy to make and are a healthy dessert option when topped with honey. You could also make the cornbread in a 9x13 pan and cut them into squares.

Potatoes
Butter
Sour cream
Chives
Salsa
Cheese
Broccoli

Sabbath Cornbread

1 ¼ cups cornmeal   ½ teaspoon salt
1 cup flour   1 egg
¾ cup brown sugar, packed   1 cup buttermilk
¾ cup white sugar   ¾ cup oil
1 teaspoon baking soda

In a bowl, combine dry ingredients. In another bowl, beat wet ingredients. Stir the dry and wet ingredients together until just moistened. Fill muffin cups ¾ full. Bake at 425 degrees for 12 to 15 minutes. Cool 10 minutes before removing and serving.

Day Four — Hot dogs, beans, veggies, and s'mores

A note from Gennifer: Kids love camping food! Prepare your preferred type of hot dog (Veggie Links, etc.) and add baked beans and carrot sticks as a side to round out the meal.

S'mores made with graham crackers, marshmallows, and a chocolate square add a nice camping touch. Our kitchen staff made s'mores in the oven in just minutes. They had all the ingredients stacked in pre-made s'mores on baking sheets and just popped them in the oven to let the chocolate melt and the marshmallow to get soft. Hot chocolate is another great option.

Hot dogs (we planned ahead and bought institution sized can of Linketts)
Buns or sliced bread
Mayonnaise
Ketchup
Mustard
Vegetarian baked beans
Carrot sticks
Graham crackers
Marshmallows
Chocolate

Day Five — Pizza, carrot sticks, and dessert

A note from Gennifer: With children, it seems pizza is always the party food of choice. To bring home the point of heaven being the specialist Celebration place ever, we do pizza on the night we focus on Heaven.

A note from Sonja: We were blessed by generous church members who gladly purchased take-out pizza for each of our Friday night VBS programs. This was always a special treat to bring in Sabbath and it fit well into each Friday night program. Kids generally find treats, like take-out pizza, just as, or more special than a gourmet meal!

There are several options here. You can order pizza as a special treat if your budget allows. You can buy frozen pizzas and prepare them. Or you can make pizza buns. Open up hamburger buns or English muffins on a baking sheet, top with marinara (red spaghetti sauce), sliced olives or other toppings, and cheese. Bake or broil in the oven (watch closely if broiling; it will burn easy).

Carrot sticks are a quick way to add nutrition and are good dipped in ranch dressing. White cupcakes for dessert are a reminder of heaven. You could also use angel food cake.

Pizza
Carrot sticks
White cupcakes or angel food cake

Day One — Barefoot Tag

Materials:

- Some "dirty" areas in the playing field where the children will have to run through. It can be mud, tempera paint, or fine dust. It just needs to be something that will make their feet dirty.

- Buckets or basins of water (one for every two children)

- Hand towels (one for each child)

Instructions:

Divide children into groups of about 10 to 15. Have all of the children take their socks and shoes off and place in a safe area. Designate an adult/teen leader for each group. Designate one child to be the "shepherd." Tell the children they are going to play a game similar to tag. The designated "shepherd" will try to catch a "sheep." That sheep then becomes the new "shepherd," and so on for the allotted time for the game.

Following the game, the children should gather by the game leader. The leader will assign each child a partner. Groups of three are allowed if there are an odd number of children. The children will then be given instructions on washing each others feet. An explanation of why this is significant is as follows.

Explanation:

This week is about celebrations! Tonight is a time to remember that with Jesus we are saved for life, and because of Him, tonight is a celebration of freedom from our sins. When we play, we get dirty, but when we go to a party, we get all cleaned up and dress nice. When we want to be part of Jesus' celebrations, we do the same thing, inside and out. When we let another person wash our feet, we show Jesus we want our heart to be clean, too. When our heart is clean, we are saved for life, and we are ready for all the celebrations life brings us!

Day Two — Hide and Seek

Materials:

- Baskets (one for each team)
- Artificial fruit/groceries (10-20 items per basket)

Instructions:

This game can be played outdoors if space and weather permit. Prior to the game, adult leaders should hide the contents of their fruit/grocery basket in an area designated for their team.

Once the children arrive for the game, divide them into teams of about 10 and assign them an adult/teen leader. The team leader will say "ready, set, go," and the children will run to their designated area and search for the food items. Once they find an item, they need to run back to their basket and deposit the food into the basket.

The team that finishes first can encourage the other teams. If additional time remains, the kids can take turns hiding the items in the baskets and searching for them again.

Explanation:

We often think of food as the stuff of life, especially children. This is a fun game that reminds us that Jesus is the true stuff of life who hid for a three days in the grave but was resurrected to give us life!

Day Three — Relay Race

Materials:

- Copy of the Ten Commandments for each team (leader to use as needed for review or help)

Instructions:

Divide children into teams of about 10. Place half of the group on one end of the field (about 50 feet apart) and the other half on the other end of the field. Child number one runs down the field to their teammates on the other end of the field and is prompted by the team leader to say the first commandment.

Once child number one has said the first commandment, he or she "tags" the next child in line. Child number two runs back to the other end of the field and states the second commandment before tagging the next child in line. This continues until all children have run in the race. The commandments may be repeated if there are more than 10 children in a group.

Please note: The knowledge of the children will vary, and some children will need more prompting than others. Younger children, or those with less knowledge of the commandments, may need to repeat all or part of the commandments rather than say them on their own. Team leaders may choose to review the commandments prior to the game. The point of this game is to encourage the memorization of the Ten Commandments, however that can be accomplished.

Explanation:

Latter fruits, or Pentecost, is a day that God came near to His people and talked with them. We will be learning about the most important words God said during this celebration. When we listen and know God's words, they become part of us. God's words in us give proof of life from God. We can learn more about what our heart looks like when He is living in it.

Day Four — Red Rover

Materials:

- An open playing field
- Designated lines

Instructions:

Designate one child to be the "announcer." The announcer stands on one side of the playing field. All of the other children stand on the other side. The announcer will say:

> "Red Rover, Red Rover, Send all believers _____ over."
> For example, "send all believers wearing red over" or "send all believers with brown hair over."

Everyone who meets the designated criteria tries to run to the safety line on the other side of the field without being caught by the announcer. Those who are caught join the announcer in trying to catch the next children to run. The game continues until all children are "caught." The game can be repeated several times with new announcers as time allows.

Explanation:

Sharing life is hard to do if you are the only one. Life is much more enjoyable when we are together and can celebrate as one big group. When we are together, we make an impact on those around us. Just like in the game when the group was larger, it was easier to catch people so that the group continued to grow.

Day Five — "Moving Camp"

Materials:

- Camp items (ideas listed below)
- A wagon for each team
- Stakes to mark next camp site
- A whistle for each team

Instructions:

Divide the children into camps of 10 to 15 children. Have camps set up for each team that include some or all of the following items:

- Sleeping bags
- Simple children's tents
- Traveling hats/clothes
- Rolls of blankets
- Backpacks/suitcases
- Pots and pans
- Food
- Water bottles/canteens
- Toothbrushes/personal care items

Mark several additional areas with stakes. The team leader will blow a whistle. This is the signal for the teams to "pick up camp" and move to the next campsite. Children will need to try to get everything moved to the next campsite before the whistle is blown again. Team leaders can allow 2-5 minutes for teams to move items depending on the number of children participating and the number of items used.

A note from Sonja: My children, along with Gennifer's and many others in our church family, are very familiar with camping. However, the type of "camp" set up in Bible times is very different from what they are used to! A short explanation/ discussion of modern verses talking about the early "camping" of the Israelites may be interesting for the children. They may not realize that the Israelites did not camp in RV's with full hook ups or tents with cooking and sanitation facilitate close by!

Explanation:

Some days we love camping, but after a time of camping, it's always good to come home. Similarly, there are many wonderful things on this earth, but the good life awaits us in heaven!

Day One — Saved for Life!

Page:	Hear ye, Hear ye! The king and queen enter!
	(The king and queen enter and sit in royal chairs.)
King:	What's on the agenda for today?
Queen:	I don't know. You're the king; you tell me.
King:	Let's call the jester and ask her. *(rings bell; Jester comes in)*
Jester:	You rang???
King:	What's on the agenda for today?
Jester:	Well, first you should brush your teeth and hair, not with the same brush, then make sure you're not wearing jammies. In fact, I would put on the royal court attire—
Queen:	*(coolly)* I would hope the jester can see we have attended to those matters already!
Jester:	Oh, of course, but I was asked what was on the agenda, and first things first.
King:	Well, then what?
Jester:	Well, I would make sure your laundry is caught up—
Queen:	*(stiffly)* Really? We have other people to help us with that.
Jester:	Well, you did ask …
Queen:	Actually, that was the king, but since this conversation needs help, I'll ask. What is the agenda at court today? Wait, why are we asking you? Why would you know? Where is our royal calendar and its royal keeper?

Jester: I think the keeper left …

King: Why would he do that?

Jester: Because there are too many celebrations this week! It's just overwhelming to a person of that nature. I, of course, could easily handle that many celebrations in a day, let alone a week.

Queen: And how would you handle them?

Jester: A party—games, food, friends, surprises!

King: Like this week?

Jester: Exactly! Like what our wonderful VBS team planned for us!

Queen: So what else do you know?

King: Our celebration today is about the Passover.

Jester: Passover? I thought it was about being *saved for life*.

King: Exactly!

Queen: I understand throwing a party in celebration of being saved from something, but what does the Passover have to do with anything?

King: Didn't you listen to our story today?

Queen: *(loftily)* I was occupied.

Jester: I'll tell you all about it, right after this. Right now it's time for the celebration to continue! I'm *saved for life*!

Day Two — The Stuff of Life!

(The skit starts with the king and queen sitting on their thrones looking at magazines.)

King: So, what's today's celebration?

Queen: I'm supposed to keep track? I thought you gave that job to someone.

King: *(rings bell)* Oh yes, where is our jester. I mean our new calendar keeper?

Jester: *(arrives lugging a big box)* You rang?

Queen: What's the party for today?

Jester: I think we have to cancel today's party.

King: What? I thought it was parties all week!

Jester: *(points at box)* I think there are more important things than parties all the time.

Queen: I agree.

King: Like what?

Jester: We need to think about things like the *stuff of life*. I read this book last night about what we need to live: food *(pulls out a candy bar)*, water *(pulls out a water bottle)*, warmth *(pulls out a blanket, shivers a little)*, and air *(pulls out a full balloon)*.

King: And parties.

Jester: That wasn't in there.

King: What about the balloon?

Jester: *(hugs balloon)* This is for my air!

Queen: I think it would work better for a celebration.

King: *(excitedly)* Celebrations! I knew there was a reason for a party!

Queen: *(picks up and opens a nearby folder)* And look, today is about the *stuff of life*.

Jester: I'm all ready then! *(holds up appropriate item at the correct time)* I have my food, my water, my—

King: Your balloon!

Queen: Actually, these celebrations are about Jesus. We need Jesus for eternal life.

Jester: Oh, I get it! Jesus is the *real stuff of life*. We need Him way more than all of this! *(motions at pile of "life" stuff)*

King: I knew there was a reason for a party today!

Jester: I can't believe I forgot to put Jesus in my *stuff of life* box.

V   B   S
Director: Well, just don't forget to put Him in your life, in fact, let's do that right now.

Day Three — Proof of Life!

(The king and queen are getting ready to play a game. Some of the pieces are set up on the board, and the queen is reading the instructions out loud.)

Jester: *(comes running in happily)* I am ready for today!

King: What's the special occasion?

Queen: Are you sure?

Jester: *(energetically)* Yes, I am sure! Today is all about *proof of life*, and as you can see, I have life! *(does hand stand, cartwheels, or jumping jacks)*

King: *(abstractedly)* Yes … we can see that …

Queen: So tell me about this *proof of life*. Is it this show of, ah, excessive, I mean, ah, abundant, energy?

Jester: No, it's more than having energy. I think that life needs rules.

King: So does this game we are playing, but I don't remember what they are!

Queen: *(waves the rule sheet at the king)* I'm working on it!

Jester: Some games are easier then others. I have this older brother who plays chess. Talk about crazy rules!

King: Talk about crazy rules—at least you had an older brother. You know what kind of rules little brothers make for the games you play with them?

Queen: I don't think I got an answer to my question …

Jester: Oh, yeah, well I was watching this thing about getting eight hours of sleep at night, eating fruits and veggies at meals, and a bunch of other things at my big sister's house.

King: And watching this information gave you all this, ah, energy?

Jester: Well, maybe. But I thought I would try following what it said. What do you think?

Queen: I always had good success with that kind of thing. I would say your results are typical.

King: *(studying the game pieces)* Sounds better then what my little brother would come up with.

Queen: So what does this have to do with today's celebration?

Jester: Oh, yeah. Today is a celebration about when God gave us—the Ten Commandments and the Holy Spirit, our Comforter, and I was trying to figure out why that was a reason to celebrate, but then I figured out!

King: That would be exciting!

Jester: Like I said, life needs rules, and we need help learning the rules.

Queen: If life didn't have rules, what would you do? Drive on the wrong side of the road?

Jester: Well, I wasn't talking about the game of life. I was talking about us and our relationship with God. But that was really good. You should have like, like, a really important job since you know so much.

Queen: Thanks, but I thought being "queen" was important.

King: That all depends on the king and what he's king of …

Jester: Ha, ha, funny. I guess the same is true with rules. It depends on who makes them. That's why I want to follow Jesus' rules.

Queen: *(looking at the game and directions again)* I think I've got it! *(pointing to the king)* You go first!

Day Four — Sharing Life!

(The king and queen are sitting on their thrones, but they look sleepy. They have night caps on and pajama bottoms and slippers peeking out from under their royal robes. They are clutching teddy bears and resting their heads on pillows. The Jester is sleeping on a blanket or sleeping bag on the floor, snoring softly.)

King:	Oh, I am so tired!
Queen:	Well, if you hadn't tried that ridiculous stunt maybe you wouldn't feel so tired.
King:	Me? That was the jester!
Queen:	The jester! You were the one who laughed so hard you choked!
King:	But it was the jester who started to eat her pillow!
Queen:	And who tried to feed her a slice of cardboard?
King:	*(starting to laugh)* If the jester had thought her pillow was a marshmallow, she should have been thankful to have the graham cracker to go with it! *(Jester gives a big snort in her sleep.)*
Queen:	That was very bad of you!
King:	*(laughing harder)* I was afraid the feathers in her pillow would tickle her the rest of her life. I saved her from a terrible outcome! *(The jester hugs her pillow and then turns it toward her mouth and pretends to take a huge bite. After chewing contentedly for a few seconds, she puts her head back down on the pillow and continues sleeping.)*
King:	See, she is at it again. What are you going to do about it?

Queen: I will give her a bite of my very healthy dairy free, sugar free, chocolate free, gluten free, pectin free, carob Life protein bar to go with her marshmallow dreams. *(The queen produces a large chocolate bar wrapped in a LIFE wrapper.)*

King: *(laughing, he is bent over and holding on to his middle)* All right, you try!

(Queen runs over to the jester just as the jester makes another attempt at biting the pillow. The queen puts the bar in the jester's mouth just as the jester opens it to take a bite. The jester bites off the chocolate, chews it, and with a contented smile, snuggles back into sleep.)

Queen: *(walks back to the throne and speaks to the king)* See, I told …

Jester: *(jumps up and makes chocking sounds while holding onto her throat and looking around wildly)* What was that terrible thing I ate? I was dreaming about a nice fat, white, soft marshmallow *(hugs pillow)*, but when I bit into it, it tasted terrible—like mouse poison or something!

King: *(still laughing)* That was one of the queen's special protein bars!

Jester: Of poison?

Queen: I thought I would save you by *sharing life* with you!

Jester: *(pouting)* It did save me from even thinking about dreaming of food again!

King: There is a better way of *sharing life* with others. Think of all the things we have learned about this week about life. We are saved for life with Jesus; Jesus is the stuff of life; and He gives us proof of life! Think of all the ways we can share!

Jester: Well, all that would sure be better then trying to poison your faithful Jester!

King: *(still laughing; turns to talk to the queen)* Oh, much better, than eating a pillow.

Jester: *(incredulously)* Does the queen do that?

Queen: *(smugly)* I can't help it if the jester has poor taste!

Day Five — The Good Life!

(The king, queen, and jester are all sitting together looking at magazines on any of the following topics: travel, pet, food, flowers, rocks, building.)

Queen: Look at this beautiful house! Fantastic!

Jester: Think that's cool? Look at these! I just love salamanders! I am going to have three pet ones in heaven with a water fountain and awesome red and blue frogs.

King: Salamanders? Frogs? I don't think I will visit your house too often.

Jester: What kind of pet will you have?

King: A kitty, just a kitty. Well, maybe some people will call it a leopard, but in heaven it will just be a kitty.

Queen: A kitty, huh? I want a house big enough that all my friends from all over can come visit me.

Jester: Even from Vacation Bible School?

Queen: Of course, especially all of my favorite people from VBS!

Jester: Even me?

Queen: Yes, you too.

King: Me, too?

Queen: Yes! Enough about that. What do you want to do with Jesus?

Jester: I want to sing a song with Jesus. A beautiful song.

King: You sing?

Jester: Well, mostly in the shower. I don't want to embarrass anyone with my beautiful voice. But in heaven, it will be different.

Queen: I want to go back to school. Imagine taking science classes with God as your teacher! Or history with the people who have lived it. I can't wait to meet Moses and Jonah and Esther, you know she is a fellow queen like me.

King: I want to walk on the streets of gold with my angel and Jesus and hear stories about when I used to get into trouble and needed to be rescued!

Jester: Oh, that will take a long time!

Queen: Give the rest of us a chance!

King: I'm going to eat all my favorite foods, too! Cooks from India, Norway, Africa, Mexico, and all over the world will have the best ingredients to work with. Wow! I can hardly wait!

Jester: Save us some, greedy!

Queen: Oh, there will be plenty for everyone. This will be the biggest celebration ever! I can't wait until the *good life* with Jesus in heaven! See you there!

Program 2

Short Stories

Parables of Jesus

Daily Schedule

	Day One	Day Two	Day Three	Day Four	Day Five
Theme	Jesus finds us	Jesus gives us choices	Choosing Jesus	Jesus gives us worth	We give to others
Main Point	I am Jesus' lamb	I have choices	I choose Jesus	I am valuable because of Jesus	I can give
Bible Story	Parable of the lost sheep	Parable of the sower	Parable of the wise man and the foolish man	Parable of the lost coin	Parable of the Good Samaritan
Crafts	Tie-dye T-shirts	Decorated flower pots	Sand art jars	Painted canvas bags	Cookies, survival kit, and/or quilt
Food	Potato celery soup and marshmallow snack mix	Burritos	Potatoes and cornbread	PB&J sandwiches, chips, and apples	Pizza and cupcakes or angel food cake
Storytime	Stories Jesus Told (The Lost Sheep)	Stories Jesus Told (The Two Sons)	Stories Jesus Told (House on the Rocks)	Stories Jesus Told (The Precious Pearl)	Stories Jesus Told (The Good Stranger)
Games	Sheep Herding	Parachute fun	Water balloon toss	Treasure hunt	Good Samaritan relay race
Skit	The Sheep Farmer	Gourmet Gardener	The Foolish Sandman	The Talents	The Good Stranger

The goal for Short Stories is to introduce children to a few of Jesus' parables. Nick Butterworth and Mick Inkpen's book *Stories Jesus Told* sparked the creativity for this program. The fun illustrations and text in the book kept the attention of all ages and yet stayed accurate and true to the earlier reading of the Bible. This book was a gift to each child at the close of VBS.

A note from Gennifer and Sonja: We love the book by Butterworth and Inkpen and decided to use multiple parables for days two and four. This allowed us to continue to use stories from this book during the second story time and still highlight our main point during the initial Bible reading.

Opening Program

Day One — Jesus Finds Us

Bible Story and Main Point:

- Parable of the lost sheep (Matthew 18:11-15 or Luke 15:4-7; also use Isaiah 53:6)—I am Jesus' lamb

Story Props:

- Stuffed sheep

- Shepherd's rod

- Numeral 99

Songs:

- "The B-I-B-L-E"

- "I Just Want to Be a Sheep"

Day Two — Jesus Gives Us Choices

Bible Story and Main Point:

- Parable of the sower (Matthew 13:3-8)—I have choices

Story Props:

- Seed packets
- Watering can
- Small pot

Songs:

- "The Shrink Song" (this is to the tune of "Fishers of Men" on Miss Brenda and the Kids' Time Singers)
- "I Have Decided to Follow Jesus" (Miss Brenda and the Kids' Time Singers)

Day Three — Choosing Jesus

Bible Story and Main Point:

- Parable of the wise man and the foolish man (Matthew 7:24-27 or Luke 6:47-49)—I choose Jesus

Story Props:

- Hammer
- Umbrella

Songs:

- "Sandy Land"
- "Wiseman"

Day Four — Jesus Gives Us Worth

Bible Story and Main Point:

- Parable of the coin (Luke 15:8-10 and Matthew 13:44-46)—I am valuable because of Jesus

Story Props:

- Coins
- Wallet or purse
- Checkbook
- Chocolate coins
- Fizzy water

Songs:

- "Seek Ye First"
- "The Joy of the Lord" (Miss Brenda and the Kids' Time Singers)

Day Five — We Give to Others

Bible Story and Main Point:

- Parable of the Good Samaritan (Luke 10:30-37)—I can give to others

Story Props:

- Bandages
- Water bottle

Songs:

- "The B-I-B-L-E"
- Kid Favorites

Crafts

Day One — Tie-Dye T-shirts

Materials:

- Plain white T-shirts (one for each child)
- Fabric dyes in multiple colors (a kit with soda ash is recommended)
- Rubber bands

Optional Materials:

- Thick cardboard to make stencil
- Spray paint for painting plastic (available anywhere spray paint is sold)

Instructions:

Prepare the dye in tubs or large buckets by following the package directions. Have the dye ready before class begins. Once the children arrive, help each child select a shirt appropriate for his/her size. Then have the children roll up their shirts and wrap rubber bands around them to make a pattern. Next, dip the shirts into the tubs with the dye, allowing some dry time between colors. Finally, hang the shirts to dry.

A note from Gennifer: You can personalize the shirts before VBS at a low cost. Simply make a stencil out of foam poster board. You can preprint your phrases using a computer and large font. We sprayed "Short Stories Inc., 20__" onto each shirt. Do this part outside! Place a piece of poster board inside the T-shirt, and place the stencil on top. It does help to anchor the stencil. Spray paint over the stencil! This is an extra step and will need to be completed by an adult, but it is a great way to remind the children of VBS and get others to ask them about their shirt.

Explanation:

Every sheep is unique and special to its shepherd, just as you are unique and special to God. Today you are going to make your own tie-dyed T-shirt, which will be just as individual as you are.

Day Two — Decorated Flower Pots

Materials:

- Small to medium plants (one for each child)
- Small to medium clay pots (one for each child)
- Permanent markers
- Water bowls
- Tempera paints in various colors
- Paint brushes

Instructions:

Kids love to plant things, and making their own pot makes this activity extra special. Give each child a pot and write his/her name on the bottom with a permanent marker. Encourage the children to decorate their pot with the paints on the table. Once their pot is done, set it aside to dry.

You may also choose to plant a plant, or you could do that later after the pot is dry. You can buy cheap plants at a variety of places, but it is also very likely you can find someone who would love to donate the plants. Spider plants grow prolifically and work great, but there are many other types of plants. The plant doesn't have to be large; children are happy with having a plant of their own, and a small plant fits a small pot, which was less expensive.

A note from Sonja: My girls loved their spider plants so much that they insisted on keeping them in their bedroom following VBS. This was a great way to start teaching responsibility, as they had to remember to water the plants each week.

Explanation:

Today you get to decorate your very own pot for a plant. Before VBS ends, you will take your pot home filled with a beautiful plant. You will need to take special care of this plant, just as Jesus cares for you.

Day Three — Sand Art Jars

Materials:

- Empty baby food jars (one for each child; you can usually collect these from church members or look for them at thrift stores; small canning jars can also be used, but they require more sand; you may also choose to buy sand art containers directly from Oriental Trading)

- Craft sand in a variety of colors (available from Oriental Trading or craft stores; we are also told that a cheap, easy way to make colored "sand" is to use plain table salt mixed with dry tempera paint until you achieve the desired color and texture)

- Small funnels (one for each child or children can share)

- Permanent marker

Instructions:

Place sand in small to medium pourable containers on the table. When the children arrive, give each one an empty baby food jar and place their name on the bottom and their lid with a permanent marker. Then allow the children to pour the sand into the jars using a funnel. Encourage the children to make patterns and fun lines with the sand. It is very important that the children fill the jar all the way to the top so that the shape they made holds its pattern.

Explanation:

What better way to remember a sand story than to create a craft with sand! Remember, you want to build your life on Jesus, the Rock, not on the slippery sand.

Day Four — Painted Canvas Bags

Materials:

- Small canvas bags (one for each child; available at Oriental Trading or craft stores)

- Fabric markers in a variety of colors

- Plastic cups to hold markers

Instructions:

Place the fabric markers in cups on the tables. Give each child a canvas bag, and encourage them to decorate the bag as they choose. Suggest decorating with pictures and sayings that remind them of their value to God. Remind them of the story they heard earlier. Younger children may need to just decorate freely.

Explanation:

We are valuable to God. This canvas bag will hold stuff that is valuable to you. When you carry the bag to Sabbath School or school or the store, remember how much God loves you and how special you are to Him.

Day Five — Cookies, Survival Kit, and/or Quilt

There are several options for day five. You may decide to do one or several of the options.

Cookies

Materials:

- Cookie dough (store bought or homemade)
- Rolling pins
- Baking sheets
- Cookie cutters
- Frosting (if desired)
- Sprinkles (if desired)

Instructions:

Allow the children to make and/or frost cookies. If the children are making the cookies, help them roll out the dough. Then give them cookie cutters of various sizes and shapes to cut out the dough. Next, place the cookies on pans and bake them in the oven. Allow the children to frost the cookies at a later time, if desired.

We thought making something to share would be nice, and we thought that a dozen small children making and frosting sugar cookies would be a good idea! You can try it if you want, but if your VBS children are small, you might decide to do what we did, which was kinder to the "stranger," and have the children eat the cookies instead of giving them away!

Explanation:

It's fun to make things and give them to others. Making cookies for someone else is a "sweet" way to share God's love with another person.

Survival Kit

Materials:

Plastic bag and each of the following items (one for each child)

- Toothpick
- Rubber band
- Bandage
- Pencil
- Eraser
- Chewing gum

- Penny or mint
- Candy Kiss
- Tea bag
- Sheet of paper explaining the "whys"

Instructions:

Have each child build a "Daily Survival Kit" using the supplies provided. Place each item in piles on a table, and have the children move along and fill their bag with one of each item. These items are just suggestions. You can find many more online if you search for "Daily Survival Kit" items.

Explanation:

Today is about giving to others, and we are going to make a great first aid kit to give to others for helping with all kinds of hurts.

Following are the "whys" for each item and a relevant scripture to accompany them. Copy and include in each kit.

- Toothpick—to remind you to pick out the good qualities in others (Matthew 7:1).

- Rubber band—to remind you to be flexible. Things might not always go the way you want, but it will work out (Romans 8:28).

- Bandage—to remind you to heal hurt feelings, yours or someone else's (Colossians 3:12-14).

- Pencil—to remind you to list your blessings every day (Ephesians 1:3).

- Eraser—to remind you that everyone makes mistakes, and it's okay (Genesis 50:15-21).

- Chewing gum—to remind you to stick with it, and you can accomplish anything (Philippians 4:13).

- Penny or mint—to remind you that you are worth a mint (John 3:16, 17).

- Candy Kiss—to remind you that everyone needs a kiss or a hug every day (1 John 4:7).

- Tea bag—to remind you to relax daily and go over your list of blessings (1 Thessalonians 5:18).

Quilt

Materials:

- Fabric quilt pieces and ribbon ties (you can order this quilt craft from Oriental Trading with the pieces pre-cut and the ties provided)

- Fabric markers

- Plastic cups to hold markers

Instructions:

Give each child a fabric square. Allow the children time to decorate their square with the markers provided. Encourage them to decorate the quilt with reminders of their favorite times at VBS. After the squares have dried, an adult can tie the quilt together at the corners and hang the finished piece. The kids will be so excited to see the finished product!

A note from Sonja: We hung our completed quilt in the church foyer for several weeks. This quilt is still proudly displayed in my Kindergarten Sabbath School room over a year later!

Explanation:

A small fabric quilt is a lot of fun to make, and it is a great way to share VBS with our congregation and show them the fun things we've worked on this week!

Food

Day One — Soup, bread or crackers, and marshmallow snack mix

Any favorite soup recipe can be used, but following is our favorite potato celery soup recipe. Serve the soup with bread or crackers.

For dessert, prepare the marshmallow snack mix. The marshmallows in the mix are a reminder of the sheep in the Bible story for the evening.

Potato Celery Soup

10–15 potatoes, peeled and diced	2 teaspoons salt
½–1 bunch celery, chopped	1 tablespoon butter
1 large onion, chopped	2–3 cans celery soup
	1 carton sour cream

Place the potatoes in a large cooking pot. Put some celery and onions in a blender and cover with water. Blend and pour over potatoes. Repeat as desired to minimize chunks. Cook until all is tender. Add the rest of the ingredients and serve.

Marshmallow Snack Mix

Small marshmallows	Peanuts (check for allergies)
Raisins	Coconut (check for allergies)
Chocolate Chips	Any other items you desire

Mix in a large bowl, and place in small cups to serve.

Day Two — Burritos and dessert

Bean burritos are an easy and filling meal, and kids love filling tortilla wraps with the fillings they choose! Just have everything in an assembly line, and you are good to go.

Flour tortillas (we had both large and small sizes available, which were warmed)
Refried beans (we bought the no-fat refried beans in the can and served them warm)
Cheese, shredded
Lettuce, shredded
Tomatoes, diced
Green onions, cut
Black olives, sliced
Sour cream
Salsa
Avocados or guacamole

Day Three — Potatoes, cornbread, and dessert

You can bake or boil the potatoes. Our staff thought boiling them was easier. We used many of the leftovers from the previous meal idea to make a potato bar.

Cornbread is a great addition to this meal. Following is my all-time favorite cornbread recipe from my brother, Peter, who loves to make things special. Mini cornbread muffins are easy to make and are a healthy dessert option when topped with honey. You could also make the cornbread in a 9" x 13" pan and cut them into squares.

Potatoes	Salsa
Butter	Cheese
Sour cream	Broccoli
Chives	

Sabbath Cornbread

1 ¼ cups cornmeal	½ teaspoon salt
1 cup flour	1 egg
¾ cup brown sugar, packed	1 cup buttermilk
¾ cup white sugar	¾ cup oil
1 teaspoon baking soda	

In a bowl, combine dry ingredients. In another bowl, beat wet ingredients. Stir the dry and wet ingredients together until just moistened. Fill muffin cups ¾ full. Bake at 425 degrees for 12 to 15 minutes. Cool 10 minutes before removing and serving.

Day Four — PB&J, fruit, chips, and dessert

A note from Gennifer: My husband, Jeremy, packs a lunch similar to this one, and my boys always want to eat Daddy's lunch stuff! The days I let them pack a lunch and eat outside like Daddy are so special! Today's meal is special because each child can pack their own lunch, too!

Make peanut butter and jam/jelly sandwiches and cut in half. Bag the sandwiches in sandwich bags, most of the bags should only have half a sandwich since it is better for the kids to come back for more versus wasting food. Place the sandwiches on a tray or baking sheet.

Similarly, place chips and sliced apples in baggies. Place each food group on a different tray ready for pick up. Put brown paper bags out in place of plates. Let each child put a sandwich, chips, etc., in their bag and eat on blankets on the floor, inside or outside.

Whole wheat bread
Peanut butter (check for allergies)
Jam or jelly (we did grape jelly and strawberry jam)
Chips (you can buy big bags and divide into individual servings or just buy chip snack packs)
Sliced apples (sprinkle with Fruit Fresh to prevent browning)
Dessert

Day Five — Pizza, carrot sticks, and dessert

There are several options here. You can order pizza as a special treat if your budget allows. You can buy frozen pizzas and prepare them. Or you can make pizza buns. Open up hamburger buns or English muffins on a baking sheet, top with marinara (red spaghetti sauce), sliced olives or other toppings, and cheese. Bake or broil in the oven (watch closely if broiling; it will burn easy).

Carrot sticks are a quick way to add nutrition and are good dipped in ranch dressing. White cupcakes for dessert are a reminder of heaven. You could also use angel food cake.

Pizza
Carrot sticks
White cupcakes or angel food cake

Day One — Sheep Herding

Materials:

- "Sheep," also known as balloons or tennis balls (one for each child)

- Permanent markers

- "Shepherd's staffs" (one for each child; can use old wrapping paper rolls, swimming noodles, rolled newspaper that is taped, or sticks)

- Rope or string to mark off a "corral"

- Obstacles such as chairs, pillows, blankets, etc.

Instructions:

Before the game, draw a face, feet, and tail in permanent marker on each balloon or tennis ball. (Our Jester went so far as to name each sheep and write its name on the tummy). Also, set up obstacles between the starting line and the roped off corral where the children are supposed to "guide" their sheep to.

When the children arrive, give each one a "sheep," and tell the children that they are going to pretend they are shepherds. Show them the rods and tell them that the object of the game is to be the first shepherd to get his or her sheep into the fold with the rest of the sheep in the rope corral. Tell them that anyone caught hitting someone with their rod will have to sit out of the game. Have the children stand at the starting line with their sheep between their feet. The first child to push their "sheep" across the floor with their "rod," avoiding all obstacles, and reach the "gate" is the winner of that round.

This is a fun chance for the children to pretend that they are a shepherd like in the story! The children will enjoy facing a new challenge when getting their sheep safely into the fold. Normally sheep follow, but today they will have to be pushed!

Explanation:

You will have your very own "sheep" to help get home to its sheep pen. And even though it is only a balloon/ball, it will be special to you because it's yours. You are so special to Jesus because you are His, just like the shepherd's lamb is special to the shepherd.

Day Two — Parachute Fun

Materials:

- "The Shrink Song" (the words are in the Music section)

- Game parachute (borrow from a school or buy from a school supply store or online) or a large colorful sheet

- Soft balls, such as those for play pits, etc. (optional)

Instructions:

Have the children stand around the parachute or sheet, hanging on to an edge or handle. Play "The Shrink Song" and have the kids slowly "grow" when it says "grow-grow-grow" and slowly shrink when it says "shrink." You can move in a circle when it says "read your Bible, grow every day." You may choose to shake the parachute and do other movements as well.

You can also place balls on the parachute and start on the ground and say, "One, two, three, GROW!" Once you say grow, everyone stands up and tries to toss the balls.

You can also play the "switch spots" game. Pick two kids at a time to switch spots by running under the parachute. You can tell them to pretend they are running for the "good soil."

Explanation:

This game is a good way for children to visualize the concept of Bible reading and growth in a physical way! Remind children of the parable of the seeds. Tell them they are going to play a game where they get to be the seeds and grow!

Day Three — Water Balloon Toss

Materials:

- Empty water / soda bottles
- Pea gravel or small rocks
- Sand
- Water balloons (five for each child)

Instructions:

Fill water balloons and tie. Place the filled balloons in a large plastic container for easy transport to the starting line. Fill five bottles full of pea gravel. In another five bottles put some sand in.

Make a start line. Set bottles up on benches about twelve feet from the start line where the kids will stand. Explain that the bottles with the rocks represent the house on the rocks, which will be harder to knock over. The other bottle represents the house on the sand, which will be easier to knock over because there isn't much sand in the bottles.

Allow each child a turn to throw their water balloons at the bottles.

Explanation:

Think about how much stronger rocks are than tiny grains of sand! They make a much better foundation for a structure, just as Jesus makes a much better foundation for our lives than anything else! Today we are going to play a game to show the strength of rocks and the instability of sand. Think about the strength of Jesus in your life as you play this game.

Day Four — Treasure Hunt

Materials:

- Child's small wading pool

- Large package of pet bedding wood chips

- Treasures (we used a jar of spare change, some candy coins, and a few small things with Bible verses on it, such as pencils)

- Paper lunch bags

- Markers

Instructions:

Fill the wading pool with pet bedding, sprinkle the treasures over the top, and gently stir everything together. Have the children put their name on a bag, and allow the children to gather around the pool and dig for treasures. This is a fun activity that gives the children a chance to find their own treasures!

Explanation:

Treasures are special and fun for everybody. Even more fun and special is when you find a treasure that was hidden or lost. Today you are going to find some special treasures of your own. And, remember, you are Jesus' special treasure!

A note from Gennifer: Who doesn't love a treasure hunt? I remember back to when I was a small child and the little town I was from had a coin hunt in a pile of sand—even finding a few pennies was such a thrill because of the hunt. Recreating that feeling was what I was after with this game. Now you know how God feels about you—you have value because God gives you worth!

Day Five — Good Samaritan Relay Race

Materials:

Supplies per team—should have at least two teams playing at the same time:

- Water bottle with water or water in a cup

- 3 bandages

- 2 ace bandages or strips of fabric

- Small blanket

- Cuddly stuffed animal

Instructions:

Form teams of four children each. It's good to have one adult coach per team. Explain that this is a relay to help a "hurt" person on your team.

Choose one person from each team to be the hurt man who was robbed and beaten on his way to Jericho. Have the hurt people lie on the floor at the end of the room opposite their teams. Give each team their supplies for the game.

On "go" a team member races to take one of the items to the "hurt" person. Once the child has given the "hurt" person the item, he/she returns and tags the next member on the team, who takes the next item. Team members waiting for their turn can cheer their team members on.

The race continues until all of the supplies are used. Play this game several times with the children taking turns being "hurt" and running.

Explanation:

Use this game to illustrate how Jesus wants us to take care of each other. Once every team has accomplished this, read aloud Luke 10:25-37. Ask, "How did you feel when you were helping the hurt person? If you were the hurt person, how did you feel while you were being helped? How would you feel if you were hurt like the man in the parable and no one stopped to help you? What do you think Jesus meant when he said, 'Love your neighbor as yourself'? What can you do to help others in need?"

A note from Gennifer: We planned our games for outside, but one day it rained. We used all the action songs we could find on our CD and got the wiggles out. We played musical chairs, "Father Abraham," and "The Shrink Song." We also made an obstacle course using chairs and whatever else was handy! It was unplanned, but so fun! Having a backup plan is a good idea.

Day One — The Sheep Farmer

(King and queen seated; Jester enters)

Jester: And how are you doing tonight, my fine king and queen?

King: What? Did I call you? *(to queen)* Did I call this clown?

Jester: I'm not a clown!

King: Why are you in my royal presence—

Jester: *(interrupts)* But I just read the most marvelous story! I had to tell you! Wait tell you hear this!

Queen: We could wait till morning when you are supposed to be here.

Jester: But, see, there was this farmer. What a great farmer! Well, actually he was a rancher, well, I don't know—he had sheep! Maybe he was a farmer… Anyways, he had one hundred sheep! Except one day he was counting *(counts 1, 2, 3, 4…)* and all he had was 99 sheep.

King: So what? Ninety-nine sheep is enough sheep for anyone!

Jester: No, because every single sheep was important to the farmer—especially the sheep that was lost. A wolf *(growls and snaps)* could eat it. A storm could come and rain on it *(make rain sounds and shiver)*. Poor, cold shivering thing.

Queen: *(addressing king)* Dear, this clown is making me cold. Hand me a blankie, please.

(King hands queen a blankie and hot water bottle.)

Jester: The farmer—or was he a rancher? Sorry, I just can't remember, and it's bugging me. Do you think a guy with sheep is a rancher?

Queen: Ugh, a smelly farmer.

King: No, a rancher. You know, if I wasn't a king, I would be a cowboy! Yee-haw! *(slaps the queen on her leg)* Giddy-up, cowboy! Whohoo!

Jester: As I was saying, the farmer had to go find his sheep! No hill was to tall, no river to cold.

Queen: You mean deep?

Jester: There are some cold rivers out there. Neither sleet, nor rain—

Queen: That's the mail service.

Jester: Whatever the case is, the rancher was looking for his sheep. He called and called, Wooly!! Wooly!!! He looked high and low, up and down *(look appropriately)*. His back hurt, it got late, his head hurt, he was tired, his feet hurt.

King: Why couldn't he just be happy with his 99 sheep?

Jester: The farmer had to find his sheep! Then he heard a sound. Was that his sheep? Yes. It was! It was his lost sheep! He grabbed his sheep *(grab a child)* and threw it around his neck *(pick the child up if you can)*. And he carried it home! Here's the best part, then he had a huge party!

(Play party music for a few seconds.)

King: Because he was finally home?

Jester: No, because the lost was found! The Bible tells us that Jesus is the Shepherd, and we are like sheep, and when we choose Jesus' there is a huge party because the lost is found.

King: I want a huge party!

Queen: I want to go to bed.

Jester: Oh, it's not a farmer or a rancher—it's a shepherd! I love these stories! *(Leaves reading the Bible)*

Day Two — Gourmet Gardener

(The scene starts with the empty throne room. The jester comes in singing or humming softly. The jester carefully tries out the king's chair, as if buying it for a lot of money. Then the queen's chair, once again very carefully. Finally, the jester flops into one chair and uses the other as a footstool. Just then the queen comes in. When she sees the jester, she stops suddenly, shocked! The king, following close behind, bumps into the queen and stands, looking shocked, too.)

Queen:	What, may I ask, are you doing sitting in the royal seats, clown?
Jester:	*(with a pouty face and sad voice)* I'm not a clown.
Queen:	Whatever you are, you better get out of my seat.

(The jester moves out of the queen's seat but is still in the king's seat.)

King:	*(pointedly)* What are you doing?
Jester:	I was just reading my Bible before bedtime *(holds up Bible)*, and I realized I have choices! See, in this story I was reading, Jesus was talking about this guy, and he planted seeds…
King:	Oh, I love seeds and planting and gardening—not weeding—but eating the yummy food from the garden is good. Did I tell you about the stir-fry I made from all the stuff in my garden? Talk about choices. What to put in the stir-fry was quite the choice.
Jester:	Yes, well this guy picked out seeds *(looks over the children, and picks out four who you've already talked to about the skit)* and took them out to the garden and planted them so carefully because he loved them so much.
King:	Yes, I know.

98

Jester:	Except, some of the seeds fell on ground by some birds, and the birds ate the seeds before they could even grow!
	(Take one "seed" back to their seat.)
King:	I hate birds!
Jester:	Some of the seeds grew where it was rocky and dry, and when the sun was hot, they just … didn't do so good.
	(The king sinks down and sits on the floor.)
Jester:	And some seeds were where the thistles grew, and they got… ah… choked. *(Take another "seed" away.)*
Queen:	I think this guy should get a clue and find a new hobby. That would be a good choice.
Jester:	But get this! The seeds that went into the good part of the garden grew— they produced! The Bible says some thirtyfold, some sixty, and some a hundredfold! *(Motion for other children to join the "seeds" up front.)* One pumpkin seed—a hundred more pumpkins! One cucumber seed—sixty more cucumbers! One corn seed—thirty ears of corn!
King:	Cool! What a garden!
Queen:	Technically, I don't think you can have thirty ears of corn on one plant—
Jester:	Oh, it's a parable—it's a story to show that we have choices.
King:	*(standing)* Yes, I would like the choice to sit in my seat…

Jester: *(moving)* Oh, yeah, but about the other choices, wouldn't you want to be one of those seeds in the good ground? It says we have the choice by listening with our *ears*—get it? Ears? Corn? Anyway, by listening to what Jesus says, we can grow. Plus we help make an awesome harvest for our king. I think I'm going to get a Bible for my MP3 player; then I can listen with my ears to Jesus' words so I can keep making good choices. *(Heads off "stage" looking in a catalog.)*

Queen: *(looks to the king)* I know gardens and harvests are your kind of thing, but a hundredfold! That's a good choice. Do you want to read first, or should I? *(Picks up the Bible and starts thumbing through it.)*

Day Three — The Foolish Sandman

(King and jester are sitting on the floor playing a card game such as Uno or Skipbo, do not use poker cards. Queen comes in carrying a wet umbrella and shakes it over the kids before sitting down on her throne.)

Queen: It's so wet out there!

Jester: I was just reading about rain in my Bible. Have you heard this story? There were two friends, and when they were growing up, they were always talking about building a house. One always said he was going to build a cedar house on an island and was going to make it so nice, nicer than your castle here.

Queen: *(snotty)* Really?

Jester: Oh yeah, real nice. When he was little, he figured it would have elevators so he would never have to climb up the stairs, and he would be right on the beach so he could go swimming and have tons of rooms so all his friends could come over. And he wanted big freezers so he could have all kinds of frozen treats while he was out playing in the sand. When he grew up, he put his plan into action, and he built a beautiful home on the sandy beach. I hate to say it, but it was nicer than this castle.

Queen: *(pointedly)* Really.

Jester: Oh yeah, way nicer, with cedar walls and freezers and everything, right on an island. And all his friends came, and oh did they like his house. Well, except one. He was kind of a stick in the mud. He had built a house too. But it was one of those self-sufficient houses where you cook on a wood stove. And he had a cellar for his food and a well for water. He lived up in the mountains, and he ate different foods *(make a weird face)*. He said he was worried about the house on the island. He didn't think it was really safe to be inside or even beside it.

Queen: *(again pointedly)* Is my house safe?

Jester: Oh yeah, I mean, I *hope* so! See, I guess the guy on the island didn't have enough money to build the house on a foundation, the hard bottom part of the house, and make it nice, with the cedar and stuff, so he just skipped that part. We have a foundation, right? *(Bounces up and down on the floor.)*

King: Of course we do.

Jester: Well, the other guy did too, and he didn't know how you could build a house without one, and he didn't really want to see. Well, one day the winds blew *(motion for the kids to help blow)*, and howled *(howl and get the kids to follow your example)*, and the guy on the mountain went into his house and roasted marshmallows in his fireplace, and then he went to bed. But the guy on the island, on the sand? When the wind blew *(motion for more blowing)* and howled *(motion for more howling)*, he got a little worried. He had hoped there wouldn't be such a storm ever. Well the wind kept blowing *(motion for more blowing)* and howling *(motion for more howling)*, and guess what happened?

Queen: With that nicer-then-my-castle house?

Jester: Yep. Kids, can you all do this *(clap)* on the count of three? One, two, three *(clap together)*. Yep, that's what it did. CRASH! The Bible says GREAT was the ruin! I bet there were pieces of that big cedar house in the water for hundreds and hundreds of miles by the time that storm and the ocean were done with it.

King: *(tapping floor with feet)* I'm glad we have a good foundation!

Jester: The Bible says that choosing Jesus gives us a good foundation. But choosing to live without Jesus is like building on the sand without a foundation!

Queen: *(gasps)* I will choose Jesus!

King: Yeah, I want a good foundation! I choose Jesus, too!

Jester: No big splats? *(looks hopefully at the kids)* Do any of you want to build a really nice house on the sand and go SPLAT?!! No, we all want good foundations; I will choose Jesus, too!

Day Four — The Talents

(Start the scene with the king counting money on a small table. All the money is being sorted into piles equal to a dollar. So, a pile of one hundred pennies, twenty nickels, ten dimes, four quarters, one coin worth a dollar, and a one dollar bill.)

King: I love counting money—it makes me feel very rich!

               (The queen enters and quietly sits down)

King: *(with a sad face)* Or very poor…

Queen: Want to go to Burger King?

King: And order off the dollar menu?

Jester: *(entering)* Did I hear something about BK?

Queen: The dollar menu?

Jester: But you only have one dollar!

King: What makes you think that?

Jester: There is only one dollar there on the table.

King: There are lots of dollars here.

Queen: We can go to Pizza Hut?!!

King: Each of these piles is *only* a dollar!

Jester: But you have lots in this pile! *(Pointing to the pennies)*

King:　　　　But it's still a dollar. You would still have to buy something off of the dollar menu.

Jester:　　　What about that pile?

King:　　　　Yes, that pile is a dollar, too.

Queen:　　　*(frustrated, she grabs the dollar and stomps/jumps up and down on it)* This is still a dollar. Let's go to BK. Dollar value menu here we come!!

Jester:　　　You know, my Bible had a story about value. Because I belong to Jesus, I have value! He gave me talents to use for Him and that makes me valuable! *(addressing the queen)* You have value, like a dollar!

Queen:　　　I am worth much more than that!

King:　　　　How much am I worth?

Jester:　　　Lots because Jesus made you! He made you so special with talents just like in the story.

King:　　　　*(starts counting money again)* One of my talents is counting money.

Queen:　　　Are we going to Burger King?

Jester:　　　No, instead, let's have a party right here to celebrate because we are all valuable to Jesus. He made us, and we want to use our talents for Him.

Day Five — The Good Stranger

(Open the scene with the king looking at his choice of reading material and the queen sitting in a chair looking at a car magazine.)

Queen: Ridiculous, just ridiculous! Who would pay for a car that costs as much or more than a house? I mean, you aren't going to live in it! At least, I hope not. Who would want a Denali with seven DVD players, three mini fridges, twenty-four A/C chargers, satellite radio, TV and video—

Jester: *(interrupts conversation)* Did I here you say Denarii? I was just reading about…

Queen: Yes, isn't it wonderful. You could easily take a long trip with it—

Jester: *(breaks in)* Yes, a trip! That's what I was reading about! There was this guy, and he was going on a trip, but some other guys stopped him, beat him up, and left him for dead. They stole his Denarii…

Queen: Oh, that poor man, no money or transportation!

Jester: How'd you guess they even stole his donkey?

Queen: Donkey? Why would you haul a donkey with a Denali?

Jester: Denali? What are you talking about?

King: *(looks up and puts down his reading material)* Wait, Denali is a vehicle; Denarii is money during Bible times.

Queen and Jester: *(together)* Oh.

Jester: Anyway, this guy was in really bad shape and along comes this guy from church, but does he help? Noooo, He's worried that he might get his fingers dirty. Then along comes another guy from church, from his town, too. Does he help? Noooo. Not one little bit. Now, here comes someone, a guy you wouldn't want to be seen around town with. All a bunch of no good troublemakers—wait! He's stopping. What's he going to do? The old troublemaker!

Queen: *(worried)* Oh the poor, poor hurt man!

Jester: Yes, that's what the Samaritan guy thought, too. He stopped, washed the poor hurt guy with his own water bottle, and put him on his own donkey.

Queen: What about the Denali?

Jester: You mean the Denarii? The Samaritan used his own money—Denarii— to pay the innkeeper until the hurt guy got better.

King: What did the Samaritan get for all his troubles?

Queen: Oh, probably a big reward—maybe his very own Denali.

Jester: Yes, he did get a very good reward. He gave everything he had to help, and Jesus saw and loved his actions.

King: That's not a reward!

Queen: I suppose that's something…

Jester: Giving *is* a gift.

King: I thought the gift was the gift.

Queen: You're confusing…

Jester: I can give and that is a gift! I can give!

Notes:

Program 3

God's Most Wanted

Daily Schedule

	Day One	Day Two	Day Three	Day Four	Day Five
Theme	Faithfulness	Specialness	Friends	Protection	Home
Main Point	Jesus is a faithful Protector just like David	Jesus makes us special	Jesus is our special Friend	Jesus protects us	Jesus has prepared a wonderful home for us
Bible Story	David the shepherd	David anointed	David's friend	David and Goliath	David going home
Crafts	Picture frames	Scented bath salts	Homemade bread	Shrinky Dinks	Hat clips
Food	Chili and cornbread	Burritos	Potatoes and cornbread	Cheese sandwiches and Cowboy cookies	Pizza and cupcakes or angel food cake
Storytime	*My Bible Friends*, "David, the Youngest Boy," last section	*The Beginners Bible*, "King David" chapter with extra talking that ties in the chapter to the main point	*The Beginners Bible*, "Best Friends" chapter	*The Young Reader's Bible*, "A Giant Problem" chapter from 1 Samuel 17	*My Bible Friends*, "David, the Youngest Boy," shepherd section from 1 Samuel 15 and 16
Games	Obstacle course	Pony rides and picture taking	Relay race	Shrinking Giant	Hayride
Skit	Home on the Range!	God chooses us	Sisters forever	The Giant Horse	The Ultimate Party

The books used for the storytime section are as follows: *The Young Reader's Bible* by Standard Publishing, *The Beginners Bible* as told by Karyn Henley, and *My Bible Friends* by Etta B. Degering.

Opening Program

Day One — Faithfulness

Bible Story and Main Point:

- David the shepherd (1 Samuel 17:34-37)—Jesus is a faithful Protector just like David

Story Props:

- Shepherd's rod
- Sheep

Songs:

- "He's the Good Shepherd"
- "Foot Prints of Jesus" (Miss Brenda and the Kids' Time Singers)
- "Turn Your Eyes Upon Jesus" (Miss Brenda and the Kids' Time Singers)

Day Two — Specialness

Bible Story and Main Point:

- David anointed (1 Samuel 16:6-13)—Jesus makes us special

Story Props:

- Medal or award
- Perfume

Songs:

- "He's the Good Shepherd"

Day Three — Friends

Bible Story and Main Point:

- David's friends (1 Samuel 20:42)—Jesus is our special Friend

Story Props:

- Photograph of a group of friends

Songs:

- "You're My Brother, You're My Sister"
- "Behold What Manner of Love" (Miss Brenda and the Kids' Time Singers

Day Four — Protection

Bible Story and Main Point:

- David and Goliath (1 Samuel 17:32-37)—Jesus protects us

Story Props:

- Shield (toy or homemade with tin foil)
- Sling shot

Songs:

- "Only a Boy Named David"
- "The Joy of the Lord" (Miss Brenda and the Kids' Time Singers)
- "The Lord's Army" (Miss Brenda and the Kids' Time Singers)

Day Five — Home

Bible Story and Main Point:

- David going home (2 Samuel 7:1)—Jesus has prepared a wonderful home for us

Story Props:

- House keys or a picture of your home
- Picture of heaven

Songs:

- "We Are Walking With the King"
- "Majesty" (Miss Brenda and the Kids' Time Singers)

Crafts

Day One — Picture Frames

Materials:

- Tongue depressors
- Popsicle sticks
- Charms

Instructions:

Use two wide tongue depressors, one on the top and one on the bottom. Then glue ten popsicle sticks, placed vertically with five on each side, to make a fence. Use Western style charms, buttons, foam decorations, and/or leather lacing to decorate a corner or two, leaving the center open for a wallet-sized photo. (See more about photos on day two in the Games section.)

Explanation:

The dedicated life of a cowboy or shepherd needs no fences. Jesus' followers go wherever people need to be protected and cared for.

Day Two — Scented Bath Salts

Materials:

Bandanas (you can buy these at large retail stores or online, or you can make your own out of colorful fabric cut in large 20" x 20" squares. We did a variety of colors/styles)

- Ribbon or string
- Sandwich bags
- Epson salt
- Liquid perfume and cologne (collect leftovers from people at church or buy at a dollar-type store)
- Food coloring
- Permanent markers

Instructions:

Warning! This craft smells strong and can be very overwhelming when all the children are together and the supplies are all in use! If someone is sensitive to strong smells, arrangements need to be made accordingly.

Set up a table for the boys and one for the girls and place gender-specific scent options on the appropriate tables. Have each child chose a bandana and write their name on it. Give each child a sandwich bag. Scoop one cup of Epson salt into each child's bag. Let the children choose colors and scents to mix into the salt in their bag. Seal the bag, and let each child squish the mixture together. Finish the project by placing each child's bag of salts into their bandana and tying it closed with a ribbon or string.

At home, these bath salts can be added to bath water. Kids love the scented, colored water that appears!

A note from Sonja: This simple craft was one of my favorites! My kids loved using their new bath salts at home, and I enjoyed them, too! The bandanas also made great costume accessories for the remainder of the week!

Explanation:

Perfume was a special part of our story today. Scents will often remind us of specific people or places and bring back fond memories. Today you will get to make your own bath salts and give them a special scent.

Day Three — Homemade Bread

Materials:

- Paper lunch bags (one for each child)

- Toothpick flags (one for each child; a strip of white masking tape three inches long folded in half over a toothpick makes a flag. Make these before VBS starts, if possible!)

- Cooking spray

- Bread dough (you can buy it in the freezer section and thaw it out earlier that day, or you can make it fresh; plan on about a lemon-sized ball of dough for each child)

Instructions:

The children should wash their hands before coming in to do this craft. The children should first write their name on a tape flag and paper bag and place it in front of their workstation. Next they should hold their hands out, palms up. Spray a light coating of cooking spray on each child's hands. Then give each child a ball of bread dough.

Let each child use the remainder of the class time crafting their very own loaf of bread. When the craft time is about over, have each child place their loaf on a baking sheet with their tape flag sticking out of it. Bake the bread in a preheated oven at 350 degrees for 15 minutes. Cool for five minutes and place in marked bags for the children to take home after the closing program.

Explanation:

Children love making bread, and with bread's universal ties, what could be a better craft for a night about friendship? Friendship is about making fun memories and sharing together. Making bread with your friends and eating together is a wonderful way to make your friendship stronger.

A note from Gennifer: I always tell the story of how my mom taught me to make bread with a recipe from a friend, and I taught my friend Sonja how to make bread, who shared this great recipe with me! We made the dough from this recipe to share with our friends at VBS, where friends will bake it, and friends will eat it together!

Sonja's Amish White Bread

2 cups warm water (110 °F)   1 ½ teaspoons salt

⅔ cup granulated sugar   ¼ cup vegetable oil

1 ½ tablespoons active dry yeast   6 cups flour

Dissolve sugar into the water. Stir in the yeast, and proof until creamy foam appears. Add salt and oil, and mix. Add one cup of flour at a time while continuing to mix. Knead the dough once all the flour is added. Store covered in the refrigerator for up to 24 hours until desired use time.

Day Four — Shrinky Dinks

Materials:

- Shrinky Dinks (found at some large retail stores and most craft stores) or clear rigid package plastic (like a Barbie Doll comes in)

- Colorful permanent markers

- Craft scissors

- Western stencils or basic pictures for tracing

- Oven (a toaster oven is a nice option, but not a must)

- Small plastic snack-size bags

Instructions:

Give each child two Shrinky Dinks or two pieces of 6x6 plastic that you have pre-cut. The children should choose permanent markers and a picture or stencil to use to trace and embellish. Very small children should be helped to choose a basic shape, like a boot, star, or horse. An adult can help trace the image for them to color in.

When the plastic is ready, cut out the shape, and follow the directions for baking Shrinky Dinks or bake the shapes in the oven until shrunk and ready. When the Shrinky Dinks come out of the oven, they will be hot, so handle them carefully until they cool.

Place the finished project in a plastic sandwich bag with the child's name on it. These can be glued to yesterday's picture frame craft project, if desired.

Explanation:

Just like David saw a large thing become small in God's eyes, you will watch what some heat will do to your project. Watch an object shrink right before your eyes!

Day Five — Hat Clips

Materials:

- Small tile pieces or cut wood pieces (1" x 3" to 2" x 5" in size; available at local craft stores or check with a crafty person in your church to see if they have scrap/spare pieces available).

- Two piece spring-style clothespins

- Glue in small paper cup with a Popsicle stick for applying

- Permanent markers

- Stickers, craft ware, twine, etc. for decorating

- Spray paint (optional)

Instructions:

If desired, spay paint clothespins a couple days before use. Have the children choose a tile or wood piece and write their names on the back. Children can decorate their piece with a marker or craft pens, depending on the type of material selected. Help children glue a clothespin to the front of the tile. This clip will be used to hold a hat when the project is complete. Decorate with stickers, twine, craft wire, etc. to complete a western look. Use a small piece of craft wire and wrap under clothespin to make a hook for hanging the project on the wall. The finished product can also be used to display favorite craft projects or other small treasures.

Explanation:

Home is not just where the heart is, but where you hang your cowboy/cowgirl hat! Today you will make a special hook that you can use to hang up a hat. You can think about the amazing home that God is preparing for you in heaven every time you see you new hat hanger.

Food

Day One — Chili, cornbread or chips, carrot sticks, and dessert

A note from Gennifer: A great way to open the chuck wagon at a cowboy themed VBS is to serve chili and cornbread or chips.

Chili (we bought the large institutional-sized can of chili beans at Walmart and warmed them on the stove for a simple child-friendly chili)

Cheese

Sour cream

Corn chips

Cornbread

Cornbread

2 cups cornmeal

2 cups flour

2 teaspoons salt

1 tablespoon baking powder

1 tablespoon sugar or honey

¼ cup oil

2 ½ cups water

In a bowl, combine dry ingredients. In another bowl, beat wet ingredients. Stir the dry and wet ingredients together until just moistened. Pour into muffin tins or 9" x 13" pan for flat, crunchy cornbread or 10" x10" pan for thicker bread. Bake at 350 degrees for 20 to 45 minutes or until knife comes out clean.

Day Two — Burritos and dessert

Bean burritos are an easy and filling meal, and kids love filling tortilla wraps with the fillings they choose! Just have everything in an assembly line, and you are good to go.

Flour tortillas (we had both large and small sizes available, which were warmed)
Refried beans (we bought the no-fat refried beans in the can and served them warm)
Cheese, shredded
Lettuce, shredded
Tomatoes, diced
Green onions, cut
Black olives, sliced
Sour cream
Salsa
Avocados or guacamole

Day Three — Potatoes, cornbread, and dessert

A note from Gennifer: You can bake or boil the potatoes. Our staff thought boiling them was easier. We used many of the leftovers from the previous meal idea to make a potato bar.

Cornbread is a great addition to this meal. Following is my all-time favorite cornbread recipe from my brother, Peter, who loves to make things special. Mini cornbread muffins are easy to make and are a healthy dessert option when topped with honey. You could also make the cornbread in a 9" x 13" pan and cut them into squares.

Potatoes	Salsa
Butter	Cheese
Sour cream	Broccoli
Chives	

Sabbath Cornbread

1 ¼ cups cornmeal	½ teaspoon salt
1 cup flour	1 egg
¾ cup brown sugar, packed	1 cup buttermilk
¾ cup white sugar	¾ cup oil
1 teaspoon baking soda	

In a bowl, combine dry ingredients. In another bowl, beat wet ingredients. Stir the dry and wet ingredients together until just moistened. Fill muffin cups ¾ full. Bake at 425 degrees for 12 to 15 minutes. Cool 10 minutes before removing and serving.

Day Four — Cheese sandwiches, fruit, chips, and dessert

A note from Gennifer: Every cowboy or cowgirl needs to pack a sack lunch to take out on the range.

For a sandwich, a simple cheese sandwich with butter or mayo may be just what your little ranchers need. Ambitious kitchen crews can have the children pick up a grilled cheese sandwich "cooked over the fire" on their way through the line. Homemade "cowboy" cookies finished the sack lunch perfectly.

Whole wheat bread
Mayonnaise or butter
Cheese slices
Chips
Grapes
Cookies

Mum's No Bake Cowboy Cookies

6 teaspoons coco powder	1 tablespoon vanilla
¼ cup butter	1 cup peanut butter (check for allergies)
½ cup milk	
2 cups sugar	3 cups quick cooking oatmeal

Mix coco powder, butter, milk, and sugar in a sauce pan and bring to a boil. Stir for one minute.

Remove from heat and stir in the rest of the ingredients. Drop a tablespoon-sized ball of the "dough" onto wax paper and let stand for 30 minutes.

Day Five — Pizza, carrot sticks, and dessert

There are several options here. You can order pizza as a special treat if your budget allows. You can buy frozen pizzas and prepare them. Or you can make pizza buns. Open up hamburger buns or English muffins on a baking sheet, top with marinara (red spaghetti sauce), sliced olives or other toppings, and cheese. Bake or broil in the oven (watch closely if broiling; it will burn easy).

Carrot sticks are a quick way to add nutrition and are good dipped in ranch dressing. White cupcakes for dessert are a reminder of heaven. You could also use angel food cake.

Pizza
Carrot sticks
White cupcakes or angel food cake

Day One — Obstacle Course

Materials:

- Variety of items to set up course (see below)

- Spray paint, chalk, or tape (optional)

- Toy stuffed animal sheep

Instructions:

Set up an obstacle course, either indoors or outdoors, depending on your preference and the weather. A variety of items can be used, including tables to crawl under (can cover in blankets), chairs to go under/around, large pillows to jump over, large boxes with ends open to crawl through, poles or trees to go around. You can also use chalk or spray paint to mark a path for an outdoor course. Masking tape can serve the same purpose for an indoor course. Place a stuffed sheep at the end of the course.

Have each child start at the beginning of the prepared course and work his/her way to the sheep at the end. When the child reaches the end, he/she should hold up the sheep to signal that the next child can begin. Continue until all the children have found their "sheep."

Explanation:

This is a chance to experience the life of David the shepherd. Kids experience the challenges a shepherd like David, or Jesus, will go through to find one of his own sheep.

Day Two — Pony rides and picture taking

Materials:

- A horse or pony

- Western decorations (a barrel, trunk, wooden horse, etc.)

- Cowboy/cowgirl dress-up clothes (vests, hats, bandanas, skirts, chaps, etc.)

- Digital camera

Instructions:

This day can be as simple or fancy as you would like. We were fortunate enough to have Gennifer's sister-in-law, Alyssa, provide us with a real horse for the kids to ride! We also had the space and the helpers to make this activity possible. The kids loved it, and it was one of the highlights of VBS! If your situation allows, make arrangements with a nearby horse owner to bring in a pony or horse for the children to ride. We had two horses, but a larger group could use more. The children took turns riding the horse with a lead rope and assistance from the handler.

A word of caution: If you are privileged enough to be able to provide horse rides, make safety a priority! Consider the temperament of the horse, and make sure the handler is experienced with both horses and children. In addition, children should wear helmets and parents should sign permission slips for their children to participate in this activity. You might also want to check with your church regarding the insurance requirements for this type of activity.

If you are unable to provide live horse rides, or if you are just not up for that much adventure, set up a western photo shoot for the kids to have fun with. This is also something you can do in tandem with the horse activity if you choose. We started the little kids on the horses and had the older kids wait to have their pictures taken and then ride. This kept the kids busy and made the wait more bearable.

Use props from your decorations and costumes to set up a western-style photo background. A couple of vests, cowboy hats, bandanas, and full skirts that can be tied around the girls' waists make great costumes. A wood barrel, saddle, trunk, or even a rocking horse to sit or stand by work well as props. Take photos of each child individually. Most digital cameras have a sepia or black-and-white option in the menu. If you cannot find that camera setting, take the pictures in color. Many photo editing programs, even free ones like Picasa, offer easy photo conversion to other color tints. Most photo processors can even print your desired color. We thought sepia (that brown toned look) was best fit for the western look.

We printed wallet-sized photos of the whole group to glue on the frame they made in craft class the first day. (Watch where you print these, some places charge more then a 4x6 print!) We also had photos printed of each child and attached them to a "Wanted by God" poster. The children were given the posters on the last day of VBS.

A note from Gennifer: Of all the VBS take homes over the years, this was by far the favorite of grandparents, parents, and children. Sepia softens the photo, and costumes always endear a child. Talk about a memorable keepsake!

A note from Sonja: Depending on the skill and willingness of your photographer, you can expand on this activity to include a group photo and photos of small groups of children (and adults) at their request. We had a very talented photographer. He took great photos of my girls that are proudly displayed in our home. Keepsake photos are a wonderful way to bring up VBS in conversation. He also took a photo of me with two of my dearest friends, Gennifer and Lisa!

Explanation:

A person of royal vestige was often seen riding on a horse as compared to walking. Today is a great day to find out firsthand why! The pictures taken today will go on or with the posters showing who God's most wanted is, which is each child!

Day Three — Relay Race

Materials:

- Two sets of the following clothes:
  - King's robe
  - Crown
  - Royal-looking scarves/belts
  - Scepter
  - Nice sandals
  - Other "royal" dress-up clothes

- Two sets of the following clothes:
  - Shepherd's robe
  - Simple belt
  - Simple sandals
  - Stuffed sheep
  - Other "shepherd" dress-up clothes

Instructions:

Make a start line and divide the children into two teams. Place a set of shepherd's and king's clothing in front of each team. About thirty feet away, create a finish line for the teams to run toward.

Each team will choose a person to start the relay as the shepherd and one person to be the friend. A leader will signal the teams to begin. Once the leader says, "Go," each team's shepherd will dress as a shepherd with the help of his/her friend. The friend will then gather the royal clothes and run with the shepherd to the other end of the field where the friend will help undress the shepherd and redress him/her as a king. Both will then run back to the start with the friend carrying the shepherd's clothes. When they reach the starting line, the next two children in line may begin.

After you play the game once, have the shepherds and friends switch roles.

Explanation:

Sharing and helping others makes life easier. David and Jonathon were friends who shared with each other and were not selfish. And Jesus, our Friend, shares with us. Let's help others and share as we run this race.

Day Four — Shrinking Giant

Materials:

- Game parachute (borrow from a school or buy from a school supply store or online) or a large colorful sheet
- Soft balls, such as those for play pits, etc. (optional)

A note from Gennifer and Sonja: We love the parachute! The children were so excited to see the return of this activity from the previous year. Use a purchased or borrowed parachute or large sheet to create a memorable activity that the kids are sure to request again and again!

Instructions:

Have the children stand around the parachute or sheet, hanging on to an edge or handle. Have an adult be the first "giant." Tell the children to lift the parachute on the count of three. The adult giant will then run under the parachute and try to make it to the other side. The children's job is to try and pull the parachute down and "trap" the giant.

After the adult shows them how it's done, the children can take turns being the "giant" and running under the parachute. As a variation, two children can run at a time and switch spots on the outside edge of the parachute.

One other variation is to toss soft balls or stuffed animals onto the top of the parachute. These can represent the "giants" in our lives. Explain that a "giant" can be anything that is too difficult for a person to handle on their own. Explain that this is why we need God! At the count of three, try to shake the giants off of the parachute because with God all things are possible!

Explanation:

Remember the story of David and Goliath? Today we get to play a game where we are giants! We will bring the parachute down low, just like David brought down the giant!

132

Day Five — Hayride

Materials:

- Hay
- One of the following forms of transportation:
    - Four-wheeler and trailer
    - Tractor and hayrack
    - Pick-up and trailer
    - Several smaller hand pulled wagons (would work well if your group is primarily younger children)

Instructions:

Who doesn't love a hayride? We kept ours simple, and the kids still loved it! We used a small trailer pulled by a four-wheeler, and we took trips around the church grounds. You can do a variety of variations of this activity as they suit your situation.

First, put hay in the trailer/hayrack/wagon. Have children ride in one large group or several small groups depending on the number of children and the size of the trailer, etc.

Again, SAFETY FIRST with this activity! Remind the children of the safety rules, including staying on the wagon, no pushing, etc. This might be another item you have parents sign off on.

Explanation:

Hayrides are something you do during a celebration at a home. Yet, to go places we love, we usually have to take a trip to get there. This activity is a reminder of an upcoming trip that's part of a celebration—the second coming of Jesus when we will go home to heaven.

Skit Scripts

Day One — Home on the Range!

Lady Henrietta:	Home on the range!
Queen:	Range—desolate, bare, empty; yes, it is a range of things. Not much of a home, though. I don't know what makes the king so excited about traipsing all over the world? At least, we have made it! I told the king I would arrive first!
Lady Henrietta:	Well, he did have some business to attend to…
Queen:	And we didn't?
Lady Henrietta:	All we had was the jester and—
Queen:	And the jester wasn't enough?! I never knew how much work it is to have a jester; I thought a jester was for us—to entertain us!
Lady Henrietta:	You haven't been bored.
Queen:	No, but I wouldn't say I have been entertained, either. *(Bell tinkles)*
Queen:	*(looks toward the sound of the bell)* Coming, coming. *(Heads in the direction of the jester who is in a sleeping bag and is looking quite sick. Lady Henrietta follows.)*
Queen:	Yes?
Jester:	Thirsty.
Queen:	Lady Henrietta, dear, run and get a drink for our little jester.

(Lady Henrietta runs and gets a cup of water. Queen fusses over the jester. Upon return, Lady Henrietta hands the cup of water to the queen.)

Queen: Here you go, a nice cup of water for you.

Jester: *(moans and tries it)* Oh, oh, it's too cold. Look! I have shivers now!

Queen: Here, Lady Henrietta, run and get a cup of something warm.

(Lady Henrietta runs off and returns with another cup.)

Queen: Here, have a nice cup of hot chocolate.

(Jester weakly tries the cup. Chokes and gags. Queen jumps up and starts patting her.)

Jester: *(whimpering)* Hot chocolate! That was a boiled candy bar! Now I have third-degree burns in my throat. Owwww.

Queen: Quick, Lady Henrietta, go get her something for her throat. *(addressing the jester)* I'm sorry, you know, that's just how the king likes his hot chocolate.

(Lady Henrietta runs off and returns with a piece of hard candy.)

Queen: Here, this will soothe your throat, Jester.

(Jester takes it limply and puts it in her mouth, wrapper and all. Makes terrible faces and spits it out. Queen looks horrified.)

Jester: You forgot to take off the wrapper! Oh, my poor mouth, it might never trust another thing I put in it. And I am sooo hungry.

Queen:	*(sounding hopeful)* I think it should almost be time for tea and cookies!
Lady Henrietta:	We are on the range, my queen; I don't think we get tea and cookies out here.
Jester:	Oh, I'm so hungry. My poor stomach. You have no idea what traveling does to it.
Queen:	Well, yes we do, but I'll try and find something. I am the queen. I should be able to get some service out here. *(Goes to find food)*
Jester:	*(huddles in sleeping bag)* So cold, so cold…
	(Lady Henrietta gets a fuzzy blanket and tucks it in over the sleeping bag.)
Queen:	*(returns with an apple)* The ranch staff seem to think you should have a fruit or a vegetable.
Jester:	*(looks like she is just waking up from a cat nap)* What! You think I used to be a fruitcake and am now just a vegetable? I'll show you! I can get up, and ohh, I don't feel good.
Queen:	*(leans over and pats Jester; tries to feed her an apple slice)* There, there, I said that the ranch staff feel that you need to *EAT* some fruits or vegetables.
Jester:	Oh, you know my doctor said I need to keep my blood sugar balanced. I would think a doughnut, one with cherry filling and lots of frosting, would be better at helping out with the whole sugar thing, huh?
Queen:	Well, I think when you feel a little better you should have another chat with your doctor about your thoughts on doughnuts.

Jester: I'm so tired; I just want to go to sleep.

Queen: I'll leave you to your sleep. *(whispers)* Come, Lady Henrietta!

Jester: But I want someone to pat me.

Queen: *(Queen sighs and settles into a position where she can pat jester's back.)*

                             (Play a soundtrack or a coyote or wolf howling.)

Jester: *(jerks up at the sound)* What was that? Oh, I'm scared! Oh, save me! I don't want to be eaten by wild animals!

Queen: I'll sit here all night if you want me to, and I won't move. If anything comes it will have to deal with me.

Lady Henrietta: And if the coyote knows what's good for it, it will stay away!

Jester: *(settles down)* You won't leave?

Queen: No.

                             (Jester relaxes and soon starts to snore.)

Lady Henrietta: *(leans over and talks softly to the queen)* Why are you doing this?

Queen: Doing what?

Lady Henrietta: Taking care of the jester.

Queen: Well, who else would?

Lady Henrietta: The ranch hands, a doctor…

Queen:	Oh, they don't know how to take care of our jester! She's ours, so we take care of her.
Lady Henrietta:	She's a lot of work, and you don't get much sleep.
Queen:	Yes, but we all love her so much. You take good care of the things you love.
Lady Henrietta:	I think if something is this much work, I'd find something new to love.
Queen:	No, no, the jester is ours, that's why we love her. We love her even when she's lots of work, cuz she's ours.
Lady Henrietta:	I don't know anyone else who would take care of the jester without a lot of pay.
Queen:	Oh, Jesus takes care of us all the time, and He even paid to take care of us.
Lady Henrietta:	That is crazy!
Queen:	Jesus loves you like crazy because you belong to Him. He is our Good Shepherd, and we are His sheep.

Day Two — God Chooses Us

(Everyone is seated around the campfire hanging out. Jester runs in with a bunch of mail, including a fancy-looking letter.)

Lady Henrietta:	Hey mail! How exciting! Anything good?
Jester:	I think so. Here's at least one good one! This one's for the King…
Queen:	Why, thank you. Oh wow! It has the royal seal; it has the big stamp; it has gold edges; it has…
Jester:	It's for the king!
Queen:	It has to be opened! Let's open it!
Jester:	I never get mail. Can I open it? I would love to.
Queen:	Or I could.
Jester:	But wait; this has the royal seal, the big stamp … it's for the king! We can't open it because it isn't ours.
Queen:	Yes, but it's a very special letter, and I am the king's wife. I can open his mail. Lady Henrietta, please get an opener.

(Lady Henrietta moves to go get the opener, and then she stops.)

Jester:	Wait, I don't think you should do this…
Queen:	As I was saying, I am the king's wife. I have some authority. The letter is from his dad, who is, like, king of everything. *(starts rambling)* You know, the king is king of all the land of the sheep and all that's here in the West. And he has a lot of brothers, and they are each kind of a king over a different place.

Jester: Is there a Burger King?

Queen: Ha-ha, yes and no.

Lady Henrietta: So, what about the letter?

Queen: The king probably has to go help his big brother with his bees—

Jester: *(interrupts)* Bees? Won't he get bit? Won't it hurt bad?

Lady Henrietta: Bees don't bite; they sting.

Queen: Maybe it is about his other brother.

Jester: Oh, not the one who loves extreme lawn mowing. My allergies are horrible when we visit him. *(Looks uncomfortable and itchy.)* I would much prefer visiting the brother who drives around in a fire truck and rescues people.

Queen: Fire trucks—the king likes making fires better then putting them out, but that wouldn't be *so* bad.

Lady Henrietta: *(clears throat)* Can we just read the letter and see what it actually says, or do you want to keep playing twenty questions?

Jester: True, but what if we have to go do something I hate.

Queen: Oh, let's just open the letter.

Jester: I could be the court letter opener—hint, hint!

Queen: No it's the king's letter, and I'll open it! *(Opens it with a flourish)*

Jester: What's it say? What's it say?

Lady Henrietta:	It probably isn't worth being that excited about.
Queen:	It says… wait, I have to unfold it…
Jester:	There's that relative who loves to garden, but it's so hot there.
Queen:	*(clears throat loudly)* It says, "Dear Son Way-out-West, I have been praying and thinking, and also talking with our pastor lately. I have decided someone else should handle the family reins. At first I thought the oldest should get the reins.
Lady Henrietta:	The reins? Is he talking about the oldest getting a new horse?
Queen:	Quict, I'm trying to concentrate. This seems important. *(Queen keeps reading to herself.)*
Jester:	Why is it important who gets a new horse?
Queen:	*(Queen looks up and looks a little dazed.)*
Jester:	*(concerned)* Did I say something wrong? The news must be worse than we thought? Quick, help the queen lie down!
	(Lady Henrietta starts forward, but the queen waves them off.)
Queen:	No, no. I am just shocked, but I'll be okay, I think. His dad says after much consideration and evaluating, he is handing the reins over to the king!
Lady Henrietta:	So, the king gets to drive the royal carriage now? What's so special about that? He has a driver who does that.

Queen:	Ah, no, ah, that was a figure of speech. Actually, the king is moving up.
Jester:	We are moving to the mountains?
Queen:	No, the big house… The king will be king of…
Jester:	His brothers?!
Queen:	Everything.
Jester:	*(heavily)* Oh, I think I need to lie down.
Lady Henrietta:	That's just like our story today. I am so excited!
Queen:	It's a big responsibility to be chosen for such a big job.
Jester:	I know, but I will do my best.
Queen:	Not you—oh never mind!

Day Three — Family Forever

(Queen, the jester, and Lady Henrietta sitting on stumps/hay bales around the campfire.)

Queen:	I miss my tea and biscuits. I miss my comfy bed. I miss my loyal subjects.
Jester:	I miss the king.
Queen:	After all the care I've given you?
Jester:	You do have to admit that it would be more fun with the king around.
Queen:	Why are we out here on the range? I thought this was the king's idea. Where is he? Not here. Why are we here? I miss my special chair, I miss my special cook.
Jester	I'm here!
Queen:	I'm so lonely for my home where I fit in.
Cowgirl Alyssa:	Yeehaw, yippee! Ride 'em cowgirl! Was that a ride or was that a ride?! You know, I saw that wild bull heading the wrong direction, and I kicked it into high gear. Angel's hoofs thundered forward in hot pursuit. That bull knew he was going to have a hard time, and I chased him like…
Queen:	*(Queen starts crying. Jester pats her and starts weeping, too.)*
Lady Henrietta:	*(Lady Henrietta hands the queen and jester a tissue/bandana/ handkerchief.)*
Cowgirl Alyssa:	Why, whatever is wrong?

143

Queen:	That bull could have killed me! And I have no horse! Do you have any idea how hard it is to run in this outfit? Oh, I want to go home!
Cowgirl Alyssa:	You want to go home when you could be here? Why? Fast horses, wild bulls, great food in the fresh air, what a life!
Queen:	But it's horrible, I can't ride, I can't rope, I can't even run!
Jester:	You need something… I know! You need a horse!
Lady Henrietta:	*(doubtfully)* A horse?
Queen:	For a pet?
Jester:	No, no, we are in the Wild West. You need a horse to ride!
Cowgirl Alyssa:	I do have a beautiful horse just right for a queen.
Queen:	It would probably kick me and laugh…
Jester:	I know, you need a hat!
Lady Henrietta:	The queen does have a tiara.
Jester:	Yes, but I would laugh at a queen riding a horse with all her bling. Imagine the poor horse!
Lady Henrietta:	But someone of her royal splendor must demonstrate by example how special she is.
Cowgirl Alyssa:	I feel pretty special riding on Angel with jeans, a T–shirt, and a hat. I don't think the sparkles would help much. I think you are special because of who you are.

Jester: Out here on the range, the title of queen doesn't seem to mean much.

Jester: Jester! You jest!

Lady Henrietta: Just ask that old bull!

Cowgirl Alyssa: I know! I can teach you to be my wrangler. I'll share everything with you! I'll find you a hat, a T-shirt, jeans—the whole works. The bull will think there are two of me! It will be awesome!

Queen: Sisters?

Cowgirl Alyssa: Yeah, like sisters. Let's see, you can ride Ginger. I know I have an extra hat. I'll even teach you how to make cornbread—it's way better then biscuits!

Queen: Better then biscuits?

Jester: *(quietly)* Maybe better than her biscuits…

Lady Henrietta: Sisters?

Cowgirl Alyssa: Yeah, it's as close as friends can ever be. You will all be my forever friends, and there's nothing I won't do for you.

Jester: Hey, I know a story like that in my Bible. It's about David and Jonathon.

Cowgirl Alyssa: And think about how Jesus loves us. We are His brothers and sisters!

Jester: Oh yeah, I know that. Hey do I get a horse and hat and everything, too?

                    (The king suddenly enters and mayhem erupts. There is much excitement and hugs between everyone.)

Day Four — The Giant Horse

(Cowgirl Alyssa and the jester walk in from the field, talking, and stand around the campfire.)

Jester:	Nobody can ride Goliath. He is way too big and wild. I can't believe you are making someone ride him.
Cowgirl Alyssa:	Actually, it's Ginger, and *she* is a girl. And I don't make any person do anything, but I did offer a reward.
Jester:	Reward? To help pay for the poor person's funeral?
Cowgirl Alyssa:	That's not very nice.
Jester:	That's what I thought. I am glad we agree. So what are you going to do about it?
Cowgirl Alyssa:	Me? I thought you should apologize.
Jester:	You are the one not being nice.
Cowgirl Alyssa:	What are you talking about?
Jester:	Making other people do your work.
Cowgirl Alyssa:	I do my own work, and at least *I* work!

(King, queen, and Lady Henrietta enter together.)

King:	Hey, what's up you two? Want some popcorn? *(Offers them a bag)*
Jester:	We were just talking about Goliath.
Cowgirl Alyssa:	*(mutters softly)* Ginger.

Jester:	And how huge he is. Nobody can ride him he is so big! I bet you would have to have a special saddle to fit around that tummy! *(Turns to Alyssa)* What do you feed that creature to make it such a giant?!
Cowgirl Alyssa:	I feed *Ginger* the same thing I feed Angel, and *SHE* is just big boned.
Jester:	*(kinda muttering)* That's what some say…
King:	I would ride Ginger.
Queen:	Oh, what if you fall off of Goliath?
Cowgirl Alyssa:	*(muttering softly)* Ginger!
Queen:	You could get hurt! Oh, what would I do?
Lady Henrietta:	The king could wear your spurs and use your saddle and take your cowboy hat…
Queen:	My special cowboy hat? Oh, whatever works. Yes, of course, take my spurs and hat and saddle and water bottle.
	(Lady Henrietta runs off to get the items.)
King:	I don't really like to ride with a saddle.
Queen:	*(yells off stage to Lady Henrietta)* Forget the saddle.
King:	And I don't know how to use spurs.
Queen:	Lady Henrietta, you can leave the spurs, too.
King:	And if I use your hat, I won't see what I am doing.

Jester: Well, what are you going to take with you to meet Goliath?

Cowgirl Alyssa: Ginger!

King: I think five little carrots.

Queen: What are you going to do with those?

Jester: You are crazier then I am!

King: Just watch and see. I think you will be surprised.

Lady Henrietta: We are already surprised, I believe.

Cowgirl Alyssa: All ready then? Let's go!

Lady Henrietta: Goodbye, Sir!

Jester: I'll miss you! And I didn't mean anything awful I ever said.

Queen: *(turns and covers face sadly)* Tell me when it's all over…

(Cowgirl Alyssa and the king walk off stage for a few minutes before sauntering back in.)

Jester: Welcome back. I knew Goliath would be too big for you. See, I am right sometimes!

Lady Henrietta: *(Taps queen)* They are back.

Queen: You didn't go through with it! Oh, I was so worried!

Cowgirl Alyssa: The king did awesome riding *GINGER*. The secret to doing something scary is knowing it's the right thing to do and who's your friend.

King: You know, Ginger doesn't look that big, and she wasn't that scary with Alyssa and Angel beside me.

Jester: Oh, I get it! It's like our story today! With Jesus as our Friend and His angels beside us, we don't have to be afraid!

Queen: Awesome! I want to ride, too!

Day Five — The Ultimate Party

Jester:	I love parties!
Queen:	I love parties!
King:	I love parties!
Lady Henrietta:	Who doesn't love parties?
Cowgirl Alyssa:	You know what's the best party? When you have come home and everything is right in your life! I love those parties!
Jester:	Like having all your favorite people around… *(Grab a kid and give them a little hug)*
Queen:	Good food…
King:	Pizza!
Lady Henrietta:	Popcorn and smoothies!
Jester:	Friends!
Queen:	Like today. I loved today!
King:	Yeah, me too. But you know, the best party is yet to come.
Jester:	You mean we're having another party tomorrow?
King:	No, I'm talking about the party that Jesus will throw when we get to heaven. That's going to be the best party even. We will get to see Jesus and eat the best food, sing the best songs, and visit with the best party guests, like King David! I can't wait!

Jester: Yeah, that does sound awesome! Are all these kids invited, too?

King: Remember, everyone is invited. All they have to do is excite Jesus' free gift of salvation, and they can go home to heaven and celebrate with us.

Queen: I think that is reason enough for everyone to say, "Yeehaw!" Yeehaw!

Notes:

We invite you to view the complete
selection of titles we publish at:

www.TEACHServices.com

Scan with your mobile

device to go directly

to our website.

Please write or email us your praises, reactions, or
thoughts about this or any other book we publish at:

TEACH Services, Inc.
P U B L I S H I N G
www.TEACHServices.com

P.O. Box 954
Ringgold, GA 30736

info@TEACHServices.com

TEACH Services, Inc., titles may be purchased in bulk for
educational, business, fund-raising, or sales promotional use.
For information, please e-mail:

BulkSales@TEACHServices.com

Finally, if you are interested in seeing
your own book in print, please contact us at

publishing@TEACHServices.com

We would be happy to review your manuscript for free.